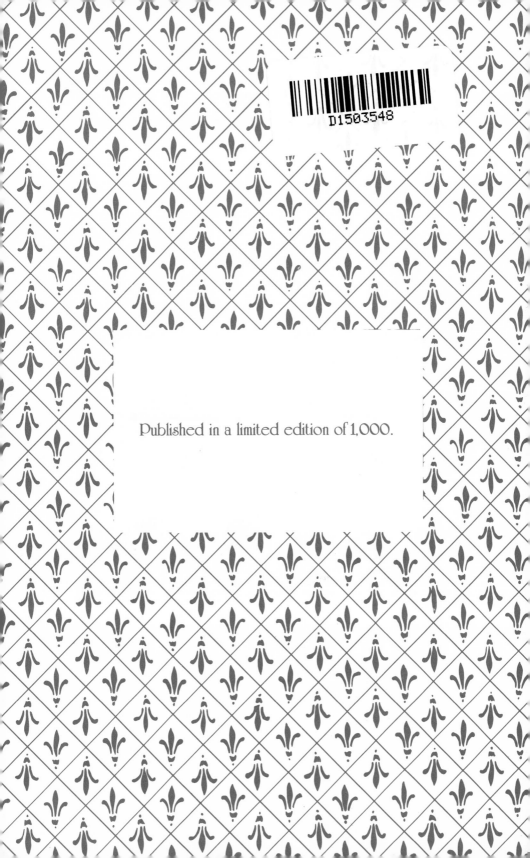

Published in a limited edition of 1,000.

SELECTED SPEECHES
OF
BRUCE McCLELLAN

SELECTED SPEECHES
OF
BRUCE McCLELLAN

ARTIFACTS
1959-1986

Edited by
Thomas Jones Johnston

Editorial/Production Supervision:
Richard Carlin

Cover and Book Design:
Main Street Design
Pennington, New Jersey

This book is printed on 100% acid free paper.

Preface

Speeches, once pronounced, are lifeless things. They may inspire, inform, depress, mobilize, reassure, those who hear them. In their rhetorical usage they obey, ideally, the Ciceronian imperatives: to inform, to please, to *move*. Nonetheless, once given, their chemistry, an intractable prisoner of time and audience, voice, bearing, engagingness, is forever lost.

It is difficult to know how perdurable will be these talks of Bruce McClellan's. When he left Lawrenceville four years ago he left behind a school and a life which were at one; his life here, a life of utterly unselfconscious giving, of service without stint or calculation, a life devoted to teachers and teaching, and to pupils, was itself his greatest bestowal. It was not what he did, but what he was, that made him, in the routinized epithet that is inescapable: a great head master of a great — perhaps indeed our greatest — school.

The words, the thoughts, the sentiments, the exhortation, the crystalline Scots-Irish bond between conscience and action (a bond so pure and so thick as to make otiose such words as "courage") that the words express — they are here on the page; and yet we must remember our cicerone in *Henry V.* We must supply with our imagination the circumstance, the setting, of the talks; remembering particularly the Chapel where many were given, the sound and echo of Bruce's voice, the house flags, the plaques, the pews, and so on; and the audience that listened rapt to what, in shy confidence, he was saying to us.

Whatever can permanently bind our community of Lawrenceville to the bestowals of Bruce McClellan must be nourished and heeded. What he gave all of us of course has been absorbed in our own lives and work, in ways that we cannot calculate. These speeches and talks remind us of his gifts to this place he has loved so well; and make explicit, once again, all that he stood out for.

Something crept into our culture around the middle of this century that makes us chary of praising and extolling those whose talents and achievements elevate them above the common run of humanity; it is often remarked that we are a hero-less culture — or that, when the young *have* heroes, their heroes are actors impersonating others, or persons who have not led, who have not displayed *character* in crisis. Bruce McClellan, the most republican of men, the most unpretentious, the most unselfadvertising, *was* a hero to this School, a truly moral man who lived and lives the ideals he knows. Our debt to him is beyond calculation.

Josiah Bunting III
Headmaster
March 22, 1990

Introduction

It is inevitable that the life of any schoolmaster is tuned to the patterns of the school year: opening days each autumn, Parents' Day, chapel services, Alumni Day, baccalaureate, and commencement. It is also inevitable that the public utterances of a Head Master are most often offered on such ceremonial occasions. During the twenty-seven years he served as Head Master of The Lawrenceville School, Bruce McClellan's remarks on these occasions, and those made in other settings, touch on a variety of subjects but tend to focus upon important occasions in the academic year and certain other topics that he felt strongly about. Therefore, I have chosen to group his remarks into five categories, giving each a title that suggests both the occasion and the focus of the remarks: "Beginnings" (convocation addresses at the beginning of the school year); "Education" (especially the importance of the residential school); "The Dignity of Teaching" (a phrase he has often used when speaking of teaching as a career); "The Divinity of Children" (a phrase reflecting his strong sense of the importance of parent-child and teacher-child relationships); and "Endings" (baccalaureate addresses and end-of-term remarks, such as at the annual Faculty Banquet).

These convenient groupings should not obscure certain themes that inform many of these remarks regardless of the category. Perhaps the single most important theme is, to use one of his favorite words, "affirmation." In his remarks, in his teaching, and indeed in his life, Bruce McClellan repeatedly affirmed the importance and value of the residential school, the dignity of teaching, the divinity of children, the worth of the individual, the sustaining values of the humanities, and the central verities of the Judeo-Christian tradition.

His words limn the character and convictions of a man of principle, one steadfast in those principles in times when many were prone to trimming. That steadfastness informed, sustained, and then led a great school for thirty-six years.

When he was approached with the idea of such a volume as this, Bruce's chief reservation was "As long as it's good for Lawrenceville." Reading the words spoken in the course of his long career, one cannot but feel that what he did, what he said, and what he is, have been, in the truest sense, "good for Lawrenceville."

Thomas J. Johnston
Lawrenceville, N.J.
June, 1990

PART I
Beginnings

September, 1956

As my text for this opening convocation I wish to use one of the most familiar of Jesus' parables:

For it will be as when a man going on a journey called his servants and entrusted to them his property; to one he gave five talents, to another two, to another one, to each according to his ability. Then he went away. He who had received the five talents went at once and traded with them, and he made five talents more. So too, he who had the two talents made two talents more. But he who had received the one talent, went and dug in the ground and hid his master's money. Now after a long time the master of those servants came and settled accounts with them. And he who had received the five talents came forward, bringing five talents more, saying, "Master, you delivered to me five talents; here I have made five talents more." His master said to him, "Well done, good and faithful servant; you have been faithful over a little, I will set you over much; enter into the joy of your master." And he also who had the two talents came forward, saying, "Master, you delivered to me two talents; here I have made two talents more." His master said to him, "Well done, good and faithful servant; you have been faithful over a little, I will set you over much; enter into the joy of your master." He also who had received one talent came forward, saying, "Master, I knew you to be a hard man, reaping where you did not sow, and gathering where you did not winnow; so I was afraid, and I went and hid your talent in the ground. Here you have what is yours." But his master answered him, "You wicked and slothful servant!"—Matthew 25:14–27

The story of the three servants is familiar to us all. My guess would be that it has been used more than any other passage in the Bible as a text for exhorting the young in school and college. There is good reason for its popularity, for the moral is both relevant and plain. Each of us—student, faculty member, and new Head Master—has a crucial responsibility to make the most of his own abilities. No other person can do it for us. We must do it ourselves.

This is a truth we all agree upon as we begin a new school year. We look forward to shining achievement, and I shall not belabor the point or do more than briefly hint that it may be possible that some of our bright resolves may

3

grow slightly tarnished after the first marking period or after the final cuts from varsity football.

What I am particularly interested in this morning is the servant with two talents. Observe that he received a reward equal to that given the man with five talents. Observe also that the master gives these two servants the same accolade, "Well done, good and faithful servant." No distinction is drawn between the two men because one started with more than the other. Both achieved excellence.

What do we mean when we speak of excellence, when we say, for example, that "the pursuit of excellence" is our chief goal here at Lawrenceville? Is excellence to be construed as belonging only to those who earn honors averages? Is excellence attained only by the starting eleven on the varsity soccer team? Is excellence reached only by those who earn a post of high distinction? The example of the servant with two talents suggests that the answer to these questions is an emphatic *no*. Excellence is a relative term. If one of you, for example, runs one hundred yards in fifteen seconds, that's a pretty poor showing. If I run a hundred yards in fifteen seconds, that's an *excellent* performance. In fact it would be phenomenal!

Clearly excellence is a matter of what you do with what God gave you rather than a matter of competitive standing with your peers. Most of us, after all, are two-talent men, but that doesn't mean that we must forego our desire to achieve excellence. Our endowments do indeed vary even within a group so highly selective as ours, but even if our abilities seem modest to us, we have a fundamental responsibility to utilize them to the fullest possible extent.

Modest success earned the two-talent servant a reward comparable to that given the five-talent man, but I suggest that in a way it was probably more difficult for the two-talent servant than for his better endowed companion. The very able have their own competitive successes to cheer them on. They sometimes win warm approval when others do not. There is an old truism that "nothing succeeds like success," and it expresses a truth that many a C student or bench-warming baseball player has observed to his own chagrin.

One of the unique strengths of the community of which we are all a part is that it offers so wide a range of opportunities for us to make the most of our diverse talents and interests. A boy of apparently modest ability is as much a part of the pursuit of excellence as any one else. The test is, as expressed by one of our most distinguished faculty members, "Has the boy done his reasonable best?"

The two-talent man had done his reasonable best and likewise should we all do our reasonable best. When we all—students and faculty members alike—can say that we are doing our reasonable best, then and then only can we say that we are engaged in the pursuit of excellence.

As I have suggested before, however, it is most difficult for the two-talent man, the average student, the indifferent athlete, or the inexperienced participant in extracurricular activities resolutely to pursue excellence as I have defined it. He is so often disappointed. His labors so frequently do not seem to earn their proper reward.

These are ancient and obvious reasons for the failure of the average boy to pursue excellence rigorously. There are, however, some relatively new pressures that are particularly hazardous to the two-talent man.

With all the opportunities that we enjoy here at Lawrenceville it is ironically true that we also have the greatest temptation to become self-satisfied. Our magnificent equipment and beautiful campus persuade us that by some magical process of osmosis we are ourselves, all of us, magnificent and beautiful! The mere presence of a clearly superb faculty persuades students that they can sit back and absorb education like a blotter. To put the shoe on the other foot, the mere presence of a highly select and well-qualified student body can sometimes persuade faculty members that a half-baked job is a real job.

The heart of the matter, however, lies in a constant self-examination of our abilities and of what we are doing, not only of the things that we do easily and well but also of the things where our skills may seem to be more modest and our responsibilities less demanding. To turn a clear eye upon ourselves we must resist the pressures for conformity and stave off the current temptations for "grade-grubbing." Only then can we become self-confident, constructive individuals.

Our own community here at Lawrenceville is only a very small part of a larger society, but I am convinced that what we do here is vitally important to American education and to American society. We have gathered here a faculty and student body second to none and facilities equally unique. Each of us has a crucial responsibility to make the most of this opportunity. For ourselves, for our school community, and for our nation, it is of paramount importance that we should be good and faithful servants to the full measure of our ability.

—From the Convocation Address

> *But Peter said unto him, Although all shall be offended, yet* will *not I. And Jesus saith unto him, Verily I say unto thee, That this day,* even *in this night, before the cock crow twice, thou shalt deny me thrice. But he spake the more vehemently, If I should die with thee, I will not deny thee in any wise. Likewise also said they all. And as Peter was beneath in the palace, there cometh one of the maids of the high priest: And when she saw Peter warming himself, she looked upon him, and said, And thou also wast with Jesus of Nazareth. But he denied, saying, I know not, neither understand I what thou sayest. And he went out into the porch; and the cock crew. And a maid saw him again, and began to say to them that stood by, This is* one *of them. And he denied it again. And a little after, they that stood by said again to Peter, Surely thou art* one *of them: for thou art a Galilean, and thy speech agreeth* thereto. *But he began to curse and to swear,* saying, *I know not this man of whom ye speak. And the* second time the cock crew. And *Peter called to mind the word that Jesus said unto him, Before the cock crow twice, thou shalt deny me thrice. And when he thought thereon, he wept—Mark 14:29–31, 66–72*

First of all we see Peter, just after the Last Supper, protesting vehemently that he would never disown his Master Jesus even if it meant his own death. Then, but a few hours later, Peter in different circumstances absolutely denies his Master not once, not casually, but three times and with deliberateness.

It would be easy to say that Peter was a coward, or a fool. There is ample evidence, however, that he was neither. The truth is that he was—to put it with discomforting bluntness—thoroughly human: just like us.

Somehow, in a few short hours, what had seemed to him a gripping reality was compromised and defeated. At the Mount of Olives, just after the Last Supper, Peter knew exactly what was important to him and what was not. He was fired to remake the world. But in the courtyard of the High Priest he elected to observe his version of the familiar maxim "When in the High Priest's courtyard do what the High Priests do."

The realization that he had betrayed his Master, as he had vowed he would not, was a grievous blow. With pain and horror he wept at the self-discovery. Providence gives few men such clear experience of their own frailty. Most of us like to think that we would ourselves be more resolute under such black and white, melodramatic circumstances. Perhaps we *would* do better than Peter, but it is a question that I would not care to pursue too rigorously. What I do wish to suggest this morning is that there are some instructive parallels between Peter's experience and our own.

To begin with, there is a parallel between the fresh, new vision that Peter had after the Last Supper and the attitude with which we come to a new school year. Today, we too have an opportunity for a fresh new vision of what we can be and do. Our opportunity to begin again, to wipe the slate clean, is unique. I know of no other circumstance that presents to us so clear a mandate to take stock of ourselves, to form new resolves, and to become different and better people. The older we are, of course, the more hostages we have given to the past, but anyone too old to feel the pulsing, germinal strength of the beginning of an academic year is too old to learn and too old to teach.

On the Mount of Olives, Peter felt within himself just such a power of new creation. His discipleship was absolute, and he knew that a new world lay before him. He was totally convinced that Jesus was his Master and that denial was impossible. Our own resolve this morning is of a less climactic nature than Peter's. For us it is not a matter of being shaken to our very depths, but if the degree of our resolve is somewhat less complete, it is no less very similar in quality. What will we make of the new resolve, new vision, and new world opening before us on this bright September morning? Will we, like Peter, deny their validity within a few hours, or days?

The question deserves examination because in a very fundamental sense it is the only important question for us today, and again Peter's experience has relevance. Possessed of a fresh vision that totally encompassed him on the Mount of Olives, Peter abandoned that conviction within a matter of hours. He sank back to old habits and bland evasions. I have already suggested that he may have done so simply as a matter of self-preservation. Why, after all, should he make it difficult for himself by telling the truth about his discipleship? Wouldn't a little white lie, or even a big lie, or even three of them be a relatively small matter under the circumstances? Such an attitude, I am sure, provides some of the explanation for Peter's action, and it is likely as well to suggest to us that lack of courage may be the Nemesis of our high resolve made on the opening day of the school year.

Peter was a brave and resolute man, however, and the full explanation goes far beyond courage or firmness of resolve. The difficulty lay, I suspect, in a fundamental fact about an individual's intentions and his relationship with his society. Would we not all have ample evidence within our experience that new resolves are really very easy to come by? One thinks, for example, of Mark Twain's well known comment about smoking: "It's easy to break the habit," he said. "I know because I have done it so many times." Or one thinks of all the resolutions he has made on New Year's Day. Or perhaps one thinks of fine and repeated resolves about writing letters home regularly or sending thank-you notes promptly. Somehow we never quite make the best of our own intentions, but it is not because we are cowards or lack resolution.

My suggestion this morning is that the fundamental problem about new beginnings is that they have a way of becoming lost or distorted. They fade even as we put them to the test. Yes, we will be unfailingly faithful about homework; we will seek consultation as soon as we need help. Then comes the second or the third day or week of school, and we suddenly find that we have been less than we had hoped to be. What has happened is that a resolve that we fully intended to honor begins to look different as day-to-day events and relationships crowd upon us. Our view becomes distorted, and we fall short of our resolve. Another way to put it is that illusions begin to cloud reality, and what we had known to be absolutely certain and vitally important somehow becomes twisted.

This confusion is something we have all experienced, and I suggest that sorting illusions from reality is the principal component of wisdom. We will all agree that wisdom is a desirable quality just as we will all agree that courage is a fine attribute, but it is too simple to say that only with courage and wisdom can we make the most of our new beginning this year.

Let me return to this matter of illusions, of distorted views. They are multitudinous in our society, and they press upon us from every side, not only here in this school community, but also in the larger society of which we are a part. Let me provide an example of what I have in mind.

Not very long ago, I briefly addressed a small group of people involved in a distinguished educational program. Students, teachers, and trustees were gathered together in surroundings which quietly gave evidence of ancient riches, well-established traditions, high idealism, and absolute security.

I will be frank and say that I felt honored to be invited to speak, but I felt also that dangerous illusions were hidden in the fabric of riches, traditions, idealism, and security. Could they not lead to false values, moribund energies, other-worldliness, and smug self-satisfaction?

It occurred to me that I had just seen two plays that might provide useful points of reference. Without much thought about it, I mentioned them. To my astonishment there was an audible gasp, a distinctly physical reaction, as I mentioned the titles. They were Edward Albee's *Who's Afraid of Virginia Woolf* and *The Zoo Story*. Most of you have probably heard something about Albee's impolite language and shock tactics on stage. Both are amply in evidence in *Virginia Woolf* and in *Zoo Story*. Neither play accepts conventional illusions about what is polite or pleasant, and both etch in fuming acid an important truth. Specifically, they say with corrosive vigor that many of us live in a world of illusions most of the time.

So firmly fixed are these illusions, so fondly held to our hearts, so dearly beloved, that we can be parted from them only by drastic measures. Traditionally, the satirists have been especially concerned with destroying illusions by ridiculing them, and it is instructive to reflect that two of the three great satirists writing in the English language have used shock tactics very similar to those which Albee employs. One thinks, of course, of Jonathan Swift and George Orwell, who sliced into the fatty illusions of their respective ages and scraped bare the often unpleasant bones of reality.

I do not propose this morning to compete with Swift, Orwell, or Albee in destroying illusions. I do hope, however, that we will recognize how probable it is that our own reaction to mention of Albee's brutal plays might be very similar to the shocked, physical gasp of that small group of teachers and students gathered in a well-heeled, highly traditional, idealistic, and very secure educational community. Secondly, I would like to point to some illusions with which we are more likely to become explicitly involved.

What about Lawrenceville's traditions of scholarship, sportsmanship, hospitality, and personal integrity? It is right to know them, to be proud of them, and to share in them. It is an *illusion* to think that because someone else created them they will support us without our lifting a hand.

Who else but we can this year create anew the climate of excitement, of interest, and—yes—of disciplined study that lies at the heart of a strong academic tradition? Who else but we can this year maintain difficult standards of sportsmanship and create with our own thoughtfulness and generosity an atmosphere of friendly hospitality? Who else but we can make anew the lonely personal decisions that lie at the heart of unwavering honesty and faithfulness?

It is too easy to persuade ourselves that all is fine with us and with our School community. Albee wrote about one of his plays that it is "a stand against the fiction that everything in this slipping land is peachy-keen." Not for one moment do I think that Lawrenceville is a "slipping land," but it most certainly will be if we allow ourselves any distorted views or any illusions about our personal responsibility to begin again. To make the School anew both individually and collectively into the fine and wonderful place that it can be, we can afford no peachy-keen illusions about ourselves.

We shall make mistakes as Peter did, and the important thing will be to pick ourselves up and see how and why we were somehow misled. We can keep bright the new creation that is before us; although we must beware of illusions. To do so we must accept our responsibilities fully and personally. We must also accept the probability of defeats in the knowledge that a defeat is principally a means of learning something about our illusions. In this context of new beginnings, of illusions, and of defeat, we can say, as Peter ultimately did, that it is our triumphs that express our humanity and our mistakes that are divine.

—From the Convocation Address

9

We gather here this morning for the opening convocation of Lawrenceville's 157th year. The faculty have donned their academic regalia; the house flags have been flourished; and the Head Master is called upon for a modicum of wisdom to begin a new year.

This is my eighth address from this lectern on this occasion. As I sat down to prepare it, I asked myself a disturbing question. I asked myself whether what I had said in previous years had really been relevant. Teachers and Head Masters are notoriously pompous and long-winded. Place them in a pulpit on an opening day and they may think of themselves as being something like Moses descending from Sinai with the tablets of stone.

Hopefully some of my earlier addresses have been worthwhile. They have dealt with self-discipline, commitment, courage, integrity, and—in general—the godly, righteous, and sensible life at school. They have been, in short, quite conventional. Or to put the matter in a less kindly way, they have tended to express thoughts that we all have anyway, thoughts that need neither repetition nor explication at the beginning of the school year.

There is a kind of irony in the voicing of high moral preachments before one must deal with facts at hand. One expression of this irony has been built into the adjective "Puritan" as we use it today. For example, we speak about the Puritan work ethic. Arthur Guiterman some years ago wrote a quatrain that expresses the opposites of high ideals and contrary practice among our Founding Fathers:

The Pilgrims landed, worthy men,
*   and, saved from wreck on raging seas,*
They fell upon their knees, and then
*   Upon the Aborigines.*

With all of these thoughts in mind, I turned to the first book of the Bible for a morning Scripture reading. I wonder how many of you have caught the phrase that is repeated there seven times? I knew it was there when I turned to Genesis, but was myself surprised to find it repeated again and again, ringing through the text with unmistakable affirmation: "And God saw that it was good. . . . And God saw that it was good." This phrase, reiterated seven times in the First Book of Genesis, seems to me to strike a chord crucially important both at this particular time in history and at the opening of the school year.

In the broadest sense, we live today in a time of great uncertainty. I sense a mood of perplexity and unease among Americans of every political persuasion. Indeed, there are good reasons for this mood. The economic situation is full of paradoxes. Important and difficult social changes are taking place. We are involved in a vexatious war seemingly impossible to resolve but equally impossible to avoid. In the face of these perplexing circumstances, we need the affirmation that the world is good. We need the affirmation that there can be joy in the human condition.

Joy is the word that I want. You know all about rules and regulations, or your housemasters will shortly instruct you. You know all about your classroom responsibilities, or your teachers will shortly fill you in in no uncertain terms. You know all about the do's and don'ts of living with your peers, or one way or another *they* will get the message across.

But has anyone talked with you about the joy that is possible in a school year? As part of God's world we have the privilege of sharing in its goodness both here and elsewhere. Nothing can be more appropriate than to suggest this morning that "joy"—a sense of collective and individual goodness in our School community—ought to be a central part of our lives this year.

Like any other abstract word, "joy" needs careful definition if it is to be meaningful. There are, for example, a number of senses in which we use the word joy to describe something quite different from what I have in mind this morning.

We are often inclined to be overjoyed by the approval of our peers, by being like everyone else. Think of the fearful anxieties of a green cardinal. Or conversely, think of the overwhelming emotion of that same green cardinal suddenly and miraculously turned bright-red like all his kind!

We are often inclined to think that we will be overjoyed by the satisfaction of some desire. That is why tradition has it that the clerks in candy stores are entitled to nibble just as much chocolate as they want. Wise proprietors know that unlimited indulgence in an appetite for chocolates is a privilege that shortly turns to ashes. We are also inclined to think that creature comforts bring joy. That is an illusion especially virulent in contemporary American life. The automobile relieves us of the aches and pains of walking. Television relieves us of the need of going outside the home for entertainment. And in case there are any aches and pains left, we can turn on the vibrator in our reclining lounge chair and watch our TV in joy and in color. What a life!

There are other kinds of spurious joy which are perhaps less obvious. For example, we can and do sometimes commit ourselves to a driving pursuit of a foolish objective. The very business of it is a kind of joy because preoccupation with one goal allows us to exclude other important and necessary responsibilities. Here on campus a devotion to Periwig hockey, or "Mad" comics can fill us with joy but ruin our work in the classroom. Whitehead wrote, "It is not enough to keep busy. One must bring one's judgment to bear on what one is doing."

Finally in this matter of spurious joys I think of the way we all try to meet our ideal conception of ourselves. My youngest son recently has been sporting a cape and imitating Batman. He has a good imagination, and so far no broken legs. *The Secret Life of Walter Mitty* is another expression of the fact that we all enjoy fantasy images of ourselves and try to work them out in our real lives. Perhaps the most adult exploration of this phenomenon that I know is Conrad's *The Secret Sharer,* in which a second-self materializes in the life of a ship captain.

Conrad and *The Secret Sharer* may seem rather distant from opening day at Lawrenceville, but in fact, there is an intimate relationship for each of us. Growing up is a delicate and difficult process, and I am convinced that one very important phase of it involves trying out different roles: the football player, the cynic, the big man on campus, the intellectual, or the beatnik. These are all roles that we play, and we sometimes have a kind of spurious joy in succeeding at our role playing.

The joy that I have in mind, however, is something quite different from acceptance by one's peers, from satisfaction of desires, from creature comfort, from the exhilaration of busyness, and from success in role playing. What I have in mind as I speak of joy this morning is a sense of right relationships, a sense as fundamental as the very beginnings of creation. As human beings, we inescapably are part of this world with all its dilemmas and questions. There can be no joy greater than the feeling that somehow in our deepest fibers we are coming to terms with the world in which we live.

This sense of rightness is what I draw from the Genesis phrase, "And it was good." Nor do I think it presumptuous to suggest this morning that each of us—student and faculty member alike—not only can seek out this sense of rightness but also will experience the joy of its discovery if only we will allow ourselves to.

Let me suggest more precisely what I have in mind in terms of our immediate world here at Lawrenceville during the coming year. First of all, I think of the joy of right accomplishment: of some specific thing well done by the student, something well taught by the teacher, housemaster, or coach. Secondly, I think of the related but slightly different joy of right growing: of growth towards new and constructive understanding and capability. For the student there is the sense of more effective participation in life. For the teacher there is awareness of a precious gift imparted. Perhaps most importantly I think of the joy of companionship in the school community. Right companionship among one's peers can be a source of great joy. This is the objective of Lawrenceville's House System. It is a central part of the Lawrenceville tradition of a friendly and constructive relationship among students and faculty.

This school community is indeed good and has in it much potential for joy, but allow me to add some cautions about the search for joy. This sense of rightness is always transient and never stable. Like a will-o'-the-wisp it moves unpredictably. Though we can experience it, we cannot pin it down. Sometimes it is won only by costly battle: bruises of a House football game, tears of bitter disappointment, and anxiety of self-examination are all part of the world that is good. Agony—which is not too strong a word for it—is part of the mechanics of joy. Through one we often reach the other, though the relationship is not inevitable. Anxiety is the name of that tension that is creative in human lives. Without it we are mere drones or beasts.

The Story of Creation in Genesis has meaning for each of us at our various stages in life. For we are *all* involved in the process of self-discovery, which is creation. What I pray for in this year to come is that we may all have moments of joy. Of joy in the sense of knowing truly what we have done and not done. Of joy in the sense of knowing what we want to do and of what we must do next. Of joy in the sense of knowing where we are going.

12

Some years ago, the late C. S. Lewis wrote a book about his conversion from rationalist atheism to devout believer. He chose as his title the phrase *Surprised by Joy.*

I suspect that Mr. Lewis was right—true joy comes always as a surprise—yet I believe also that it rests upon our understanding of right action and of our world as a good world in which we have a worthwhile part to play.

The phrase is repeated seven times. It is indeed a good world as we discover in ourselves a sense of right relationships. This is what growing up is all about. This is the act of creation that is teaching. During the year ahead my hope for each of us is that we may be surprised by joy.

—From the Convocation Address

September, 1972

Happy is the man that findeth wisdom" says the well-known proverb, but what does happiness mean? That is my question this morning.

During the summer I have been reading about utopian communities for the course that I shall teach during the winter. To see people reach out for their vision of a better world is fascinating. How can one find happiness? Every utopian community begins with that question.

It's quite possible, of course, to suggest different answers to that question, but many of these are superficial. When I asked a number of guests at a dinner party this summer to define "happiness," none of them could come up with a satisfactory answer, though we all agreed that happiness is only a by-product, secondary rather than primary, and comes to us as a gift.

Happiness seems like night vision. You can see an object better at night if you do not look directly at it. Likewise, happiness, in its fullest sense, seems to come to us without our really seeking it. Or, to look at it from another point of view, sometimes when we seek what we think is happiness, we find that the feeling we had so ardently hoped to experience is simply not there. Like the will-o'-the-wisp misleading travelers in the marsh, happiness can draw us hither and yon without ever actually becoming tangible and real, yet it can walk beside us without our knowing it.

A search for happiness energizes utopian communities. To wish for a happy school year is a legitimate objective. Not that we can avoid inevitable disappointments and mistakes. These, too, are part of any shared experience.

On the other hand, I have the feeling that adults in general, and schools in particular, often back away from the subject of happiness. Its frail flower has a hard time flourishing among the crevices of the rocky landscape of intellectual discipline, housemasters' comments, and rehearsing endless hours for a Periwig performance.

Having said that, let me add emphatically that I do not think we can create a happy school year just by making things easy, comfortable, or without pain. This is not an amusement park any more than any other school or any other worthwhile enterprise. My predecessor, Dr. Heely, once described the ideal curriculum for growing boys as "Any program of worthwhile studies, so long as all of it is hard and some of it unpleasant."

Nonetheless, I do think that positive understandings can help us to create a happy school year, and I feel also that we do too little by way of preparation and say too much afterwards when things go wrong.

So I offer this morning some thoughts about student attitudes as I sense them throughout this country during this time of change. What I hope is that we may, by looking them squarely in the face, deal with some attitudes evident among young people today.

First of all, I am much concerned by an attitude of passivity, deriving in large part from vicarious television experience. All of us can go to war, throw a bone-breaking block in a football game, or participate in a peace rally without actually leaving overstuffed chairs. The result is that like startled turtles we pull our heads into an armored, self-centered shell whenever anyone asks us to do our part.

Something in human fibre seems to respond explosively to the encapsulation of passivity. When one of us, several of us, many of us begin to reach out to touch reality somewhere, we may embark on headstrong and thoughtless courses of action. They may range from innocuous but selfish blasts of stereo sets at the sound level of a sixteen-inch cannon to the destruction of plate-glass bank windows.

In a somewhat related area we are, all of us, the victims of a language barrier which results from overkill through advertising and the communications media. Where so many words avalanche upon us from all sides, none of them has meaning, so we use far more profanity with far less thought than did our parents. Thus we make "absolute demands" that in turn are really only emphatic concerns and are not absolute at all, or even demands.

Even as we become disillusioned about conventional language skills and conventional disciplines, we head towards a society that clearly will be highly complex and technical. We desperately need the skills of language as a precise tool just when language itself is becoming debased.

Evident as well among young people everywhere is a strong vein of narcissism. This is an ancient aspect of the adolescent years, born of uncertainty about self and of unsureness about reaching out to others. People who cannot make contact become omphaloskeptics: they spend most of their time looking at their own navels.

Several years ago, the trustees and faculty prior to the opening of school saw a movie called *No Place to Stay,* which developed the theme that the finest facilities and the most elaborate plans meant nothing in a school without worthwhile human relationships. The high point of the movie came when the young man whose life was being examined reached out to touch the hand of his girl.

We reach out to touch because as individuals we can express ourselves *only* in a social context. Growing young people have special, private problems, but we are all part of a larger world. In joining that world we find ourselves. Can we pledge this morning to break out of induced passivity, pallid words, and self-centered spells to create a happy 1972-73 school year?

We will find ourselves in direct proportion to the effort that we make to be part of this school in many possible ways. Having said that, I would say also that this is by no means an easy task. That is what housemasters are for; that is what teachers are for. The adults of this community must encourage self-discovery, ways of reaching out, and seek patterns of growth and development.

Happiness means feeling that we are a part of creation. The Psalmist said, "I will lift up mine eyes unto the hills." This sentiment is not reserved for prophets and saints alone. One way or another, we are all involved in this community for the coming year. One way or another, what happens in the next nine months will become part of each of us for the rest of our lives.

I hope that the experience will be happy, even as I know that it inevitably will include mistakes, difficulties, and hurt. Win a race, master a math procedure, and feel finally what a poem is saying. Joy is not necessarily without pain.

We are surprised by happiness when it is most unexpected. It overwhelms us when we feel that in some sense we have become part of creation.

—From the Convocation Address

September, 1979

In the year A.D. 64, an older man wrote to his young colleague in a distant country. In his letter, he tried to provide friendly advice and moral support for the young man who faced an appallingly difficult task. The older man was the Apostle Paul, and he was writing to Timothy, whom he called "his own son." Timothy was then leading the church at Ephesus, while Paul restlessly traveled on into Macedonia.

The text of our Lawrenceville School hymn no. 60 draws upon two verses from the sixth chapter of Paul's letter to Timothy:

But Thou, O man of God, flee these things;
and follow after righteousness, godliness,
faith, love, patience, meekness.

Fight the good fight of faith, lay hold on
eternal life, where unto Thou are also called,
and has professed a good profession before many
witnesses.

"Fight the good fight." That's the first phrase of the hymn. I love to sing it to the music of Francis Cuyler Van Dyke, who was the school organist and who played in this chapel from the time it was built until 1916.

I confess, however, that I always have mixed feelings when hearing this hymn. The music itself is indeed grand. Here in chapel, we hold a memorial service on Alumni Day each May, and at that time, there is in this building a strong and moving feeling of being in touch with preceding generations of Lawrentians.

But the language troubles me with its implied Victorian equation of virtue with narrow religious conviction. There are implications of elitism coupled with genteel politeness and with country-club churches. One thinks of the statue of the Christian Athlete that once graced the Princeton campus and of WASP America going out to carry God's plastic truth to the benighted world. The indifference and insensitivity of this language to many different, important, and valid religious traditions is today, at the very least, anomalous. At the worst, it deeply offends significant characteristics of our School community.

Knowing that we traditionally use the hymn at the beginning of the school year, and recognizing my own ambivalence about its language, I began to look at hymn no. 60 with some care:

Fight the good *fight.*
Run the straight *race.*

17

Cast care *aside.*
Faint not *nor fear.*

Those phrases seem to me good advice from an older man to a young person whom he regards as his son. They seem to me to speak a truth to a boy or young man about to face the challenges of a new school year here at Lawrenceville. They are also good advice to a faculty member who has his own challenges to face as the year goes on.

"Fight the good fight." One way or another, most of us not only hear advice of a very similar kind, but even agree with it. How many of your parents have said in the last couple of days, "Work hard, and things will go well this year." Older boys will remember those maddening comments from their teachers, "If only he would work harder, he could earn an honors average." Then there is that easy student defense, "Yes, I could work harder, and I am going to do much better next term."

"Run the straight race." That's good advice too. It's paraphrased in a lot of different ways. "Don't cut corners;" "Obey the school rules;" "Don't lie, cheat, or steal because you will only be hurting yourself;" "If you don't do it right the first time, you'll just have to do it over again."

"Cast care aside" might at first seem a little less of a truism. Yet it speaks to the proposition that we can become worrywarts and workaholics. Both exist among our student population as well as among members of the faculty. Their effectiveness is diminished, their achievement warped by an overwhelming sense of care.

"Faint not nor fear" is excellent advice. However bad it gets, someone will be there to support you. We all have bad times. Most of them can be lived through if we just don't give up at the beginning when things first get tough, and if we are willing to overcome our *inside* fears so that we can go *outside* for help.

So those four phrases that begin the stanzas of the hymn offer excellent advice. Some of you may know the hymn well enough, however, to remember that I have left something out. There is a second phrase in each stanza, a second idea: "Christ is thy strength, and Christ thy right." That is the sum of the concluding ideas in each of the four stanzas: "Christ is thy strength, and Christ thy right." What does that mean in our confusing world? How can we respond to such a narrow statement made in language so irrelevant to atomic warfare, international inflation, and political idiocy everywhere. Many of us hear the name of Jesus Christ only when it bursts bombasting out of a frustrating or mindless situation.

"Christ is thy strength, and Christ thy right" *is* Victorian, and the phrase has little meaning for a great many of us. I am not about to try to accomplish this morning what others of greater skill and deeper conviction have been unable to achieve. Rather I would like to start at the other end of the spectrum and try to look at that phrase about Christ being a strength from a general point of view.

Whatever else that phrase may or may not mean, it says one simple thing in the context of our School hymn: fighting a fight is not by itself a good thing. Work alone has no inherent value.

As I thought about our hymn, I began to make the equation of "fighting the good fight" with working hard. Then I began to think about the word "work". My shorter Oxford English Dictionary provides four columns of definitions for this simple, four-letter, Anglo-Saxon word. The sum of the definitions is that to work is to get something accomplished. What counts is not the work as such. What counts is what we accomplish when we work. To put it in another way, there is a difference between a good fight, a bad fight, and a fight that means nothing.

What then gives value to work? Value comes from the *purposes* for which we work, the *spirit* with which we work, the *secure joy* of knowing that we are headed in right directions, and the knowledge that when all is said and done, all of us are imperfect humans and can do only as much as we can do.

Those generalizations seem to me to come pretty close to what Paul meant when he wrote Timothy and to what our School hymn means.

There is abroad in the world today—especially in our American society—the idea that we work for purely self-serving reasons. We work five days a week and then claim the reward of a weekend of self-indulgence. On this campus we study on the weekday evenings and then claim the right of a Saturday night blast. We go all out as teachers for ten months of the year and then regard the summer as our reward.

This attitude toward work is one side of a Protestant ethic that we have inherited. When Adam sinned by eating the apple, God banished him from the Garden of Eden to a land where weeds had to be pulled, garbage cans had to be emptied, furrows had to be plowed, and there were all sorts of difficult, dirty tasks that had not been the lot of man before his fall. It followed logically that if one worked hard enough, one could make a little space for himself and have a little of Eden when the burdens of work could be set aside.

There is, however, another side of the Protestant work ethic. Beginning with the Reformation, work itself became a form of worship. *Laborare est orare* is the classic phrase: "To work is to praise God." Explicitly every constructive form of human activity becomes participation in God's creation.

If I am honest with myself, I recognize both points of view in my own reaction to work. Sometimes work is difficult, unrewarding, and boring, with the result that I can't wait to be released from its obligations so that I can enjoy moments of relaxation. At other times, I enjoy what I am doing so much that I hardly feel I can call it work. Most of us, I think, swing back and forth between those extremes throughout our lives.

All this leads to a simple conclusion: most human beings experience the greatest sense of pleasure and fulfillment when they know that as a result of their own hard work they have accomplished something worthwhile. I have made a lot of shortcuts as I have moved to that conclusion, but I think that the point is valid and relevant as we begin the 170th year of The Lawrenceville School.

Fighting the good fight and running the straight race are rewarding and important experiences all by themselves. To cast care aside and to know that one can always draw upon others for support and strength is to free one's self from petty fretfulness and from the slough of despond that threatens from time to time to engulf all of us. We all need support and encouragement on occasion.

But those generalizations are not enough. The goals for which we work are important; the spirit in which we work is significant; the secure joy of knowing that we are headed in right directions can be a delight; and the knowledge that, when all is said and done, we are all imperfect humans and must hold hands with each other as we do what we *can* do are all understandings that can help us meet the year ahead with a sense of proportion, dignity, courage, and joy.

—From the Convocation Address

September, 1980

This morning, I have chosen two dramatic Old Testament readings. The first is from the Book of Exodus and tells the story of Moses seeing a miraculous burning bush from which his God speaks to him:

And the Lord said, I have surely seen the affliction of my people which are in Egypt . . . Come now therefore, I will send thee unto Pharo, that thou mayest bring forth my people the children of Israel out of Egypt.

And Moses said unto God, who am I, that I should go unto Pharo, and that I should bring forth the children of Israel out of Egypt. . . . behold when I come unto the children of Israel, and shall say unto them, the God of your fathers has sent me unto you; and they shall say to me, what is his name? What shall I say unto them?

And God said unto Moses, I Am That I Am: and he said, thus shalt thou say unto the children of Israel, I Am has sent me to you.

The second Old Testament story is also familiar. It is the story of David and Goliath:

Now the Philistines gathered their armies for battle; and they were gathered together . . . And Saul and the men of Israel were gathered together, and pitched by the valley of Elah, and set the battle in array against the Philistines. And the Philistines stood on a mountain on the one side, and Israel stood on a mountain on the other side: and there was a valley between them.

And there went out a champion out of the camp of the Philistines, named Goliath, of Gath, whose height was six cubits and a span. And he had a helmet of brass upon his head, he was armed with a coat of mail; and the weight of the coat was five thousand shekels of brass. . . . And he stood and cried unto the armies of Israel, and said unto them, why are ye come out to set your battle in array? Choose you a man for you and let him come down to me. If he be able to fight with me and to kill me, then will we be your servants; but if I prevail against him, and kill him, then shall ye be our servants, and service.

21

David was the youngest of three sons of Jesse who were soldiers in Saul's army. His father had sent him to the battlefield to take food to his brothers, and he happened to arrive when Goliath made his challenge. We all know the outcome:

And David put his hand in his bag, and took thence a stone, and slang it, and smote the Philistine in his forehead, but the stone sunk into his forehead; and he fell upon his face to the earth. So David prevailed over the Philistine with a sling and with a stone.

Why was it that of all the Israelites facing the mighty armies of the Philistines, David alone stepped forth to challenge Goliath? With a weapon in his hands that was not much more than a toy, he alone took up the challenge presented by Goliath: a giant of a man armed with the full panoply of military equipment. Why were so many of the Israelites mute, passive, and afraid?

The question is important to us because we live in a time of passivity. Like the Israelites, we are intimidated, not by a mythical giant but by many characteristics of our culture and of the world we live in. Pervasive television packages events of all kinds and sizes into clean, dispassionate, fishbowl segments of watchable pseudo-reality. We watch mountains blowing up, the starving in India, suffering, elaborate athletic events, and soap opera melodramas without involvement more significant than a gulp of Coca-Cola or a handful of popcorn. Our foods themselves are precooked, and, one suspects, for the most part predigested so that we need not even chew.

The sheer size of the many problems that we face makes us feel helpless. Energy, transportation, inflation, poverty, and national antagonisms: what can any one of us do about solving these? Complexity is likewise baffling. How can we cope confidently with the national budget, the computer age, or with the cancerous bureaucracies our industrial society has generated in both the public and the private spheres of responsibility? It is hardly surprising that we are often mute, passive, and afraid.

Turning to the microcosmic scale of opening days at Lawrenceville, we must ask the question, "What are we going to do with this year that lies ahead?" Are we going to shape what happens with an active and conscious effort like David, or are we merely going to sit back passively and watch it happen to us the way we watch a Sunday afternoon football game, slouched in an overstuffed chair?

None of us can know what the future consists of. None of us can know what lies ahead for us this year at Lawrenceville. We would all agree, however, that there will be a variety of alternatives, of roads taken or not taken, to borrow a phrase from Robert Frost. Choices will be inevitable, and even refusing to make choices will in itself become a choice. What we have to ask ourselves is whether we are willing to make positive choices and accept an active role in our own futures rather than to be satisfied with a passive role in which we as individuals simply accept what circumstances others may inflict upon us.

Mankind has long wrestled with this business of choices. Why does one person choose one path and another decide on an entirely different course? Why was Goliath the champion of the Philistines, and why was David the only Israelite who would respond to the challenge? The improbable scenario of David's fight with Goliath needs an explanation.

If Sigmund Freud were to have analyzed David's battle with Goliath, he would probably have done so in terms of ego, superego, and libido. Presented with the same facts, Freud's disciple, Carl Jung, would have spoken of dark primordial dreams. B. F. Skinner would speak of conditioned responses, and Nietzsche would focus on the act of will. All of the world's great religions also provide some explanation of acts of will, of the choices people make.

Why people do what they do is, of course, an absolutely central question. No one has ever provided a single explanation that sweeps everything else before it. Rather, I think, the various explanations that we are familiar with all have some validity and all need to be treated with some caution. For our purpose at the beginning of a school year, it is enough to say that if we do not make active decisions about our roles, we are likely to become trapped in ways that we don't like and that may well have unhappy consequences for us. We need not, for example, become victims of our fathers, mothers, or teachers. Most of all, we must not become victims of ourselves.

One kind of choice-making is evident in the labels that we accept for ourselves and place on others. A student can be a jock, a nerd, a quig, a head, a grind, or an esthete. A faculty member can be a jock, a scholar, a traditionalist, an innovator, a prophet, an oddball, or a regular guy. Any of us in chapel this morning can add labels and sublabels for both students and faculty members. We do it all the time both for ourselves and to others.

Labeling is not by itself a bad thing. In fact, it identifies members of the School community who in their different ways contribute different things and become involved in various activities. We talk a lot about community because we think it is important to have shared interests and goals. On the other hand, I would be horrified if the word "community" were to be interpreted as meaning uniformity. Though some labels are used in a negative sense, the truth is that there are many different ways to contribute to any worthwhile human enterprise.

A fine soccer team contributes as much as an elegant artist. A plodding student contributes as much as someone who is always challenging. An especially scholarly teacher brings one kind of strength to our academic life while some who are not particularly scholarly can teach in ways that are extraordinarily important. The traditionalist and the innovator each has a place, as does the occasional prophet. We need them all. Moreover, it should also be said that as each is different and each contributes, so does each of us have within ourselves a little of the qualities that the labels we use are designed to identify.

Our first Old Testament lesson told part of the story of God's reply to Moses when Moses asked for a name so that he could tell the people who was speaking to them. God replies, "I Am That I Am." That phrase is interpreted frequently, and by good authority, "I will be what I will be," and that's where we return to David. Of all the people among the Israelites confronting the Philistines, it was David alone who was willing to make a significant choice. He had been labeled: little brother, shepherd, adolescent, schoolboy. He became warrior, prince, and king because he did not allow labels to trap him.

We need not all be supermen. There are a lot of different kinds of useful human lives, but certainly we all must face the importance of taking an active role in our own lives. The words from the School hymn are: "Lay hold on life and it shall be." Lay hold on life.

We will be here in Edith Memorial Chapel this morning for about fifty-two minutes. By my calculation that is roughly one one-millionth of a century. The fraction is tiny, but it is manageable to think that in one one-millionth of a century what we do is important. If we think of a fifty-two minute convocation service, an hour's class in physics, an evening preparing for English, a moment relaxing with friends, an hour practicing crosscountry, or a bull session with a housemaster, then we can recognize that the life that we have together here at Lawrenceville is something that we have to take charge of and be active about, is something that we can in fact affect by the decisions that we make.

From one point of view, the story of David and Goliath is a poor fairy tale. Who could ever believe that a peach-fuzz boy could stand up to the hardened warrior Goliath? It was a silly thing for David to do, but he didn't know it was silly because he hadn't placed any label on himself. He must have said something like, "I will be what I will be." Someone nearby no doubt said, "There goes that crazy little kid from the mountains. He hasn't even got the proper weapons." The observation was accurate, but that was the observer's problem, not David's. David was confident because he had a good image of himself, was willing to make a choice, and was prepared to step forth because he believed in what he was doing.

We need not be David or Superman during Lawrenceville's 171st year. We need only to bear in mind the importance of making good choices and avoiding stereotypic labels. God gave us various abilities and characteristics but didn't label us. That responsibility is ours. Every choice we make will create part of both our present and our future. We will be what we will be.

—From the Convocation Address

PART II
Education

January 13, 1962

I believe implicitly in the crucial importance of education as a bulwark of democracy. With all its faults and all its foibles, the American educational system is one of our noblest achievements. In particular, our great tax-supported systems are unique in history and reflect both the ideals and the pragmatic good sense of free Americans. The older, independent institutions increasingly since 1900 have been numerically less prominent, but their contribution to the quality of American education has perhaps become more significant than ever before in terms of pace-setting and experimentation. Take, for example, the Advanced Placement Program, which is currently making such an important contribution to secondary education. It originated in a study supported by the Ford Foundation and undertaken by three colleges—Princeton, Yale, and Harvard—and three schools—Andover, Exeter, and Lawrenceville—all independent institutions making a major contribution to the growth of American education.

I happen to serve an independent, residential school and in the minds of some this fact would seem to imply purposes and attitudes that are somehow opposed to tax-supported and non-residential programs. Nothing could be further from the truth. In my view everything we do at Lawrenceville is complementary to the tax-supported school systems and is guided by the common objective of creating the very best system of education in the world. I think I may safely speak in this matter both for my colleagues of the Lawrenceville School and for independent school men everywhere.

When independent school techniques, programs, and subordinate objectives appear to differ from prevailing practise in tax-supported systems—as they have recently for example, in reading, languages, and mathematics—then the differences merely indicate the vitality of freedom, the growth potential of tension, or—to put it another way—free enterprise flexing its muscles in the sphere of education.

In my remarks this evening I wish to speak as a secondary school man very much concerned about the present international situation as it is related to teaching students and helping them become effective adults. Our schools have a primary role sustaining the qualities in our society that give it meaning. What is a school but the creation of one generation to transmit civilization to its children? Fundamentally the school is the matrix from which our culture *has* grown and *will* grow, and we who are adults have a special responsibility for it.

To develop rigorously disciplined intelligence is clearly one of the school's central tasks. This is much more than a matter of drillmaster teaching. It *begins* with an atmosphere of curiosity; it is *shaped* by the traditions of our culture; and it is *sharpened* by a willingness to examine independently whatever question may be at hand. If we confine our concerns to tidy little packages of predigested factual knowledge, we may well have discipline, but we are not likely to have much knowledge. If we freewheel through grandiose ideas without requiring their firm control or a solid foundation of fact, we are likely to produce an insubstantial vapor that is neither disciplined nor intelligent. If we insist that the young ask only the questions we have asked and examine only what we prescribe, we shall find them fragile mirror images of ourselves and lacking the toughness to meet the demands that will be uniquely theirs.

Perhaps most important of all is our awareness of the difficulty of the learning process. It cannot be and should not be easy for anyone. The errors of a classroom, unlike those of a baseball game, are often as valuable as the hits. We must guard ourselves against the temptation of thinking that when a young man has reached a plateau of achievement the job is done. Precisely at this point a rigorous training demands new tasks of greater difficulty.

The kind of teaching I have chiefly in mind has varying degrees of relevance for students of different kinds of ability. It goes almost without saying that in a population as rich and diverse as ours there are many skills and many needs. It would be absurd to contend that the narrow sector of intensive, liberal-arts book learning with which I personally am most familiar provides all the answers. The principles are the same, however, for the whole range of school objectives: from a basic reading program to vocational training or to the most sophisticated college preparatory course. What we must insist upon is an atmosphere of curiosity, a sense of the traditions of our culture, and encouragement of self-reliant independence. What I wish to see in our young people as a result of their school experience—of whatever kind it may be—is a confident awareness of the virtue and delight in doing a job well and independently.

My own experience has been primarily in residential schools and colleges. Accordingly, I think of life outside of the classroom as a major training ground. It also involves rigor and sometimes difficulty. Allow me to draw, for example, directly upon my own school experience.

Within the framework of their social life, students learn what it means to help a comrade, or to hurt him. They learn what it can cost to translate a principle into personal relationships. They learn about the shallowness of the egotist and about the boorishness of the braggart, and sometimes they learn by being both.

Clear moral values and spiritual commitment require another area of training. Our society provides plenty of evidence of indifference to moral standards, and I have no illusion that schooling alone can counteract the pervasive influence of the whole. Nonetheless, we can hold firmly to the values that we think are at the heart of our civilization. We can join in the worship that is so much a part of our tradition, and we can by example suggest the depth of our conviction.

There is nothing new in these brief remarks. Nothing new except their urgency and the positive affirmation they urge in a time of apprehension. We must not fear to affirm the importance of education to a democratic society, and in that education we must strive to transmit the strongest and finest values of our society. In the context of a troubled world situation the need has never been greater. For the future offers us limitless opportunities for disaster, or for creation.

—From remarks to the Trenton Junior Chamber of Commerce

June 3, 1962

$\mathcal{S}$olomon was born to the purple. His father, David, had served the Lord God of Israel heroically and had given power and prosperity to the Jews whom he had ruled. And now Solomon inherited the throne with all the riches and honor his father had earned. Palaces, chariots, solid gold golf tees, and dancing girls, all were his. Put in another idiom: beautiful homes, Mark IX Jaguars, unlimited bank accounts, and unnumbered vacation trips to Bermuda, all were his.

At Gibeon, the Lord appeared in a dream to Solomon shortly after his accession to the throne and said, "Ask what I shall give you." On the face of it the question is absurd. Why should Solomon seek anything from his Lord? But with a perception that has become legendary, the young king asks for the one thing which he treasures above all else. He asks his Lord for a wise and discerning mind. Not for a prosperous reign or for personal power, but—simply—for a wise and discerning mind.

Solomon's desire expresses an intensely human aspiration: the wish to know more and to use knowledge well. In seeking discernment as well as intelligence, Solomon voices our general suspicion of unbridled mental power. He wants more than shrewdness, a quick wit, and a high College Board verbal score. He wants to be a philosopher-king with both the power of knowledge and the wisdom of sound judgment.

What is a wise and discerning mind? A suitable question for a baccalaureate sermon simply because Lawrenceville is dedicated to training young men's minds. It is a question especially relevant to us because the uses and abuses of intellect have never been so apparent as they are in June, 1962.

A kind of intellectual manipulation of natural forces that we call atomic physics gives us promise of both plenty and oblivion. The flickering calculations of IBM's "750" in some respects surpass our own powers and add up to both hope and terror. Technological virtuosity allows us both to dream fondly of possessing comforts and conveniences beyond measure and to have nightmares about things possessing us.

For us, as for Solomon, a wise and understanding mind is the chief gift of God's blessing. Each of us in America in general, and in Lawrenceville in particular, enjoys abundance and power at least equal to Solomon. Had he more horses, for example, than those stabled under the hood of a 1962 Chevrolet? Could he direct dial to Montana? Had he a deep freeze to reach into at a time of crop failure?

Granted that we are kings, and that wise and understanding minds are our best hope, what do we mean? What is wisdom? What are the roots of discernment?

To begin with, the mention of wisdom immediately summons to mind the image of a bookish and bespectacled person. We are a little suspicious of him because he appears to claim a kind of superiority. Actually, he seldom makes the claim; it is others less learned who cling to their suspicions as a kind of defensive bidding. "He thinks he knows more than I do," is a compelling self-justification in egalitarian America. By implication this attitude lies at the

29

bottom of jaundiced remarks about President Kennedy's Harvard appointments. During the Eisenhower-Stevenson campaigns we heard much—and often with a sneer—about "the eggheads."

As it happens, I have a very personal interest in eggheads! Be that as it may, even a schoolmaster has to admit that the intellectual approach has serious limitations sometimes unrecognized by those who use it. Its high priests classify and categorize arbitrarily in order to reach solutions that satisfy the postulates but are inadequate to deal with concrete experience. They tend to think of the rest of the world in chiaroscuro extremes of black and white. They feel that they are little heeded and speak stridently in order to be heard. They may well be right in the first place, but they can be so anxious to play their cards that they spoil the game.

Americans are particularly suspicious of eggheads because they so often seem to find what is wrong, and so seldom to find what is right. They appear to keep life at arm's length when it should be grasped closely and affirmatively. Just as a matter of speculation, doesn't Barry Goldwater's popularity rest on his warm and positive emotional convictions as compared with the pale, impartial skepticism of the stereotyped intellectual?

We would all agree, however, that intellectual vigor and discipline are fundamental components of wisdom. We study here in school because we have within us a powerful impetus to inquire, to learn, to solve the puzzles that we see. It is a search that is as old as man, and its goal is something we call wisdom. We have seen the relationship between study and wisdom in some of the greatest individuals of our western heritage—Plato, Aquinas, Lincoln—and we rightly think of it as one root of their greatness.

The intellectual component of wisdom is a matter of direct concern to us as we study here at Lawrenceville. It is more than a kind of abstract silly-putty which can be played with like a party toy or set to one side to fill in the contours of any given container. A wise and understanding mind begins first with a well-trained competence in particular, individual responsibilities. "Doctor, Lawyer, Indian chief," runs the doggerel as we skip rope. Each of us has or will have a vocation that requires an educated ability, and this requirement is our first responsibility as we seek the wisdom that Solomon asked of his Lord. None of us can know certainly what burdens we shall be asked to bear; but we can be absolutely certain that skill in some particular field of endeavor is one cornerstone of wisdom.

Another component of wisdom is the willingness to keep on learning after our formal education is complete, a willingness to keep an open mind, always receptive to new experience and new insights. This is easier said than done. Every student here today knows that his parents do not see things the way he does. Every student knows that his parents have already made up their minds about things that are not as certain as they may seem to a jaded, older generation. What do your elders think, for example, about the twist? About Tennessee Williams? Or about lacrosse as compared with baseball?

And you, too, will inevitably become less flexible in your thinking as you grow older. You will make commitments and give hostages that will on the one hand create a needful stability and on the other tend to diminish your willingness to accept the phenomena, tastes, and perspectives of a new generation following you. It is a wise man who can always keep an open mind, who is always willing to learn new things, and who will never reject the new and unfamiliar simply because it *is* new and unfamiliar.

Just as we Americans are particularly vulnerable to hardening of the arteries because of a rich diet, so are we especially vulnerable to hardening of the mind because of our present prosperity. The things which we possess threaten to possess us. They enfold our minds and veil from us what is new and promising as the world changes. While the rest of the world races by, we are sorely tempted to sit on the sidelines preserving our laurels and resting on our dogmas. The wisdom that Solomon sought includes a mind open to experience, a willingness always to learn, and an independence of judgment unfettered by chains of the past.

Wisdom is then a matter of intellectual vigor, of well-trained competence, and of a willingness to keep on learning; but Solomon also beseeches his Lord for discernment. He wants to know what is right and what is wrong so that he can govern his people.

The question can be put simply. What is right and what is wrong? There is no easy answer to it because we never meet it in its abstract form. It involves complicated choices in our own lives; it crops up in our relationships with our society; and it very largely determines the degree to which we can be at peace with ourselves.

The Old Testament provides one answer in the Ten Commandments, which tell us in no uncertain terms what is *wrong*. "Thou shalt *not* . . ." they say, and we can agree because so few of us find these prohibitions either difficult to accept or hard to follow, at least in their obvious sense. We all know, however, that a list of prohibitions, no matter how detailed, really begs the question. Here in our School community, the faculty and deans have furnished us with our own commandments. I observe that they are noticeably more numerous than the rules that Moses brought from Ararat. I wonder whether we are proportionately more virtuous.

When the Pharisees questioned Jesus about the greatest commandment, he replied, "You shall love the Lord your God with all your heart, with all your soul, and with all your mind. This is the great and first commandment. And a second is like it, you should love your neighbor as yourself." Steeped in the knowledge of the Old Testament, Jesus takes a wholly new approach to the springs of right action. The question is not what is *wrong* but what is *right*.

It is right to understand that none of us has final answers because they remain solely within God's providence. In loving our neighbor as ourself we recognize differences as well as likenesses among us and strive to make room for both. We act in the conviction that none of us has selfish privileges that trespass upon the lives of others. Because of our humility before God's divinity and our own sense of falling short, we are patient and forbearing about mistakes and misunderstandings.

Discernment—the spring of right action—is basically a point of view. It is a positive understanding of man's relationship with his creator and with his fellow man. It is the final and crucial ingredient of the wise and discerning mind that Solomon sought as the ultimate blessing. For us today, as for Solomon more than a score of centuries ago, a wise and understanding mind is the ultimate blessing.

—From the Baccalaureate Sermon

Thank you for the invitation to share this evening with you and for the opportunity to talk briefly about education from the point of view of my own professional involvement. It was Plato, I believe, who long ago pointed out that one could judge a nation's concern for its future by assessing its attitude towards education. This is a truth that we must keep constantly before us both as parents and as citizens in a democracy. It is a truth of which I am profoundly convinced on rational grounds and to which I am increasingly attached emotionally.

In two respects I may disappoint you with what I have to say. First of all, the general subject is "how best to prepare your child for college." This seems to me an impossible topic for the very simple reason that no generalizations are adequate to guide a particular child's preparation, and even if they were, the inevitable question would arise "what college?"

The only meaningful distinction that can be made among different kinds of schools is whether they accomplish what they set out to achieve. Some are successful; some are not; some are in between. Whether it be public or private, day or boarding, coeducational or segregated, progressive or conservative, the only meaningful question about a school is whether or not it accomplishes its stated goals.

The residential concept of education goes much deeper than a mere matter of providing rooms and meals at a location convenient to classrooms. It first took shape in the late fourteenth century in England when a great new foundation was created by William of Wykeham, Bishop of Winchester. For a century or so scholars had been gathering about the great teachers living in Oxford, Cambridge, and Paris. Recognizing a community of interests, they began to live together in halls and found that somehow their communal learning broadened and became more effective. With his new foundation, Wykeham crystallized and formalized these informal arrangements, and created the first quadrangle.

On one side of the square were the chapel and great hall for meals. On an opposite side there was a library. In the remaining space were quarters for the senior fellows—the teachers—interspersed among quarters for junior fellows—the students. This plan was not so remote as it may at first seem to be. Students were from thirteen and eighteen years old, roughly the age of present secondary school boys, and the basic principles with physical appurtenances were very similar to a residential school today.

As a matter of fact, the residential institution is a unique creation of the western world since the Renaissance, and its influence has been demonstrably profound. By way of digression I might suggest that abandonment of some of its principles at the university level has recently created troubling difficulties. I speak, of course, of the Berkeley riots and of similar phenomena, but that's another story.

Fundamentally, a residential school offers to the student a multitude of opportunities for independent growth within a controlled environment directed to the broadest possible spectrum of his education: social, intellectual, and moral. That's a very long sentence, and I want to emphasize some of its facets: multitude of opportunities; independent growth; controlled environment; broadest possible aims; social, intellectual, and moral. All of these possibilities lie within the coherent community of the residential school, with the result that the whole is greater than the sum of the parts. This matter of community is something to which I shall return later.

Independence for the child is one of the things that raises the most difficult questions for parents in America where the residential school tradition is concerned. Without exploring all of its aspects, may I simply put this question forward? Isn't the chief aim of most parents in the child's years from fourteen to eighteen to make sure that he can stand on his own two feet? Or perhaps I should rephrase the question to say *shouldn't* the parent seek above all to make sure that the child can stand on his own two feet at age eighteen as he begins a college career?

I doubt very much that anyone here would argue the point. If by chance there is anyone who would like to take issue, I suggest that he try his arguments first of all on his own offspring. If young people are worth their salt, they will become increasingly independent during the adolescent years whether their parents will it or no. Only the most nefarious and harmful devices can keep a child tied to his mother's apron strings.

The question then is not so much whether or not the child will become independent, as in what environment he will make the inevitable trials and errors. What opportunities will he have for growth in this period? By whom and how will he be guided?

Provided that a residential school community is clear in its purposes and firm in its ideals, it creates a unique environment designed precisely to meet the child's needs. His academic instruction takes the center of the stage with a minimum of irrelevant distractions and a maximum of opportunity in the evening and on weekends to widen his capacities or remedy his difficulties.

His social growth is under the care of professionals who do not labor under the cross purposes of a family's inevitably major emotional involvement. At the same time, they provide variegated models close at hand. Does he need help in a perplexing phase of solid geometry? It is available. Does this problem mask new and unexpected questions about his identity? An experienced professional is at hand.

He has much to learn also from his peers. Sharing a basic purpose, but disparate in experience and background, his contemporaries have much to teach him in a community that seeks to encourage individuality but at the same time requires him personally to assume responsibility. He may be a member of student government or of the Radio Club; he may be a first bass in an informal singing group; he may be a splendid soccer player. Whatever it is, he is increasing in awareness of himself and of the world around him. He is learning where he can take his place among his fellows. The residential school has no patent upon such opportunities, but they become more available and hence more probably effective when they are not circumscribed by an 8:30 to 3:30 schedule and when they exist entirely within the context of a single, purposeful community.

The quality of coherence is especially relevant to spiritual understanding.

About nothing is it more difficult to be specific. About few things are more foolish things said. We have a reasoned tradition at Lawrenceville that differs from other fine schools, and I shall not develop here our own ideas. It can be said, however, that a residential school offers a unique opportunity for a pattern of formal religious services, of academic instruction in religion, and of personal counseling that can and does have an effective value in a crucial area.

Finally I would like to return to the nature of a residential school community. It is indeed a sort of island with bridges to the mainland of adult life, but in some ways it is far less circumscribed than those who are unfamiliar with it would expect. For one thing it is not confined by reason of its location to any particular economic, ethnic, or geographic group. Presently we have in Lawrenceville boys from forty-two states and twenty-two countries. Nor is it necessarily divorced from the important social concerns of our times.

You will gather from all I have said that I think of a boarding school as something positive in nature. Rightly conceived, it can provide a broad, coherent, and fruitfully independent opportunity for growth during the years so important to subsequent success in college.

—From remarks to the Junior League

July, 1979

What is unique to Lawrenceville and peer schools is the social challenge of our times. As Clifton Fadiman pointed out in a recent Op. Ed. article in *The New York Times*, all American schools are experiencing extraordinary difficulties because of a profound shift in our national environment. Fadiman believes that for the first time in history a society's formal educational system is operating in competition with, and parallel to, an informal educational system that is extraordinarily beguiling and effective. In Fadiman's words:

> *"On the one hand is the reality-system expounded in a book, the idea, the cultural past; on the other hand is the far more vivid and comprehensible reality-system expounded by television, the rock star, the religion of instantaneous sensation, gratification, and consumption."*

Not so very long ago, the schoolroom opened doors of experience, opportunity, and achievement. Instead many young people today see schooling as restrictive and limited. "Pop" culture threatens to beat the schoolmaster at his own game.

That is particularly true of a residential school, which seems monastic to many young people. Actions that Lawrenceville regards as dismissal offenses are freely and generally indulged in by most of the peer group without any sense of reproach or wrongdoing. That truth we are already facing to some degree and will have to face even more directly in the decade of the eighties.

The ultimate question—generally evaded in America—has to do with a school's responsibility for teaching values. High academic averages, strong College Board scores, proper dress, and good manners do not necessarily make a man, though they certainly once indicated a man who could make it in our society. A school has responsibility for the qualities of character that it encourages, but it cannot create character out of thin air, or substantially modify subsequent adult behavior by rules and regulations.

There can be no debate about the general proposition as expressed by Nancy and Theodore F. Sizer of Andover that "morality is imbedded in all formal education. The experience of schooling changes all children, some for the better, some unhappily." With some trepidation, I wish in this report to establish two propositions for the decade of the eighties in terms of responding to the moral questions that seem uppermost in so many minds.

My first proposition is that an ethical system lies at the heart of the rigorous liberal arts discipline to which Lawrenceville is committed. This is an aspect of value teaching not well understood by teachers and even less well

36

articulated by teachers or parents, let alone students. Because we are reluctant to articulate this truth, our children are ignorant of it.

Let me explain what I mean, first of all, with some examples of explicit ethical principles embedded in the liberal arts tradition. The study of history, for example, informs us about human nature and about the probable consequences of certain kinds of decisions. We speak, for example, about a Napoleon complex, about Caesar crossing the Rubicon, or we quote the aphorism that those who will not learn from history will be doomed to relive it. In each instance, the study of history produces a moral insight.

Sometimes the ethical part of liberal arts disciplines may be implicit rather than explicit. A geometry theorem means on Friday precisely what it meant on Monday. It means the same in Patagonia and Peshawar. A formula applicable to certain cases cannot be bent into something else. Tyranny is tyranny whatever cloak it may wear. An objective truth is just that: objective. No subjective consideration can change it. The Biblical ground of that particular ethical principle is that a house built upon sand cannot stand for long. Truth must rest on a firm foundation.

In a larger sense, the rigorous liberal arts tradition teaches us that an important hope for man lies in the thrill of achievement one feels after having accepted the demanding disciplines necessary to discover a truth. Mere lazy ignorance leaves us blind, fearful, and superstitious. Mere indulgence leaves us with a hangover of dissatisfaction with self.

If teachers and parents are not particularly articulate about the ethical heart of the liberal arts tradition, neither are they articulate in their statements of their own beliefs and value judgments. We are, all of us, too much consensus politicians. We like to be liked too much, with the consequence that we lack definition to the young and provide fuzzy, confusing models.

Therefore, my second proposition is that we must make unequivocal value judgments. Every moral position involves some ambiguity, but I am increasingly convinced that there are absolutes that adults must set forth boldly. Let me try to provide some examples. The world of the creative arts rests upon the truth that aesthetic sensibilities help to make life worthwhile. Our instructional program recognizes the conviction that man lives by more than bread alone. In a more mundane concern we must teach fervently that each human being is responsible for the good health of his body. As we live together, we discover again and again that humility and selflessness are right; selfishness is wrong. Honesty and integrity are virtues essential to understanding ourselves as part of the fabric of all humankind.

I have tried in the preceding paragraph to relate aspects of the Lawrenceville experience to absolute value judgments. Others may add to my list or may express the basic ideas in different ways, but if we fail to take clear and definite stands, we simply confuse our young people, who have no way of learning where we are.

Looking ahead to the eighties I see the need for Lawrenceville to express a value system both implicitly through its adherence to the rigorous liberal arts tradition and explicitly through its support of specific statements. If that makes us a monastery in the eyes of the alternative education system, so be it. We cannot try to roll back time to some presumed, former golden age. That would be an exercise in futility. Rather we must look ahead to the new kinds of challenges that face our students, our faculty, our alumni, and our country.

—From the Head Master's Report to the Board of Trustees

June 4, 1981

Well, we are here! We have arrived. This evening's baccalaureate service is the next to last stop on this particular journey for the Lawrenceville Class of 1981. As an observer has pointed out:

> *In leaving [school] we recognize our passage through time. We leave a community, friends, teachers, and part of ourselves. Learning to leave means acknowledging change, and on another level, it means that part of our lives has already been completed, finally and forever. As at other moments of significant transition and great emotion, we surround ourselves with family and ceremonies.*

Look at the flags; sense the occasion; be aware of our families gathered to share the occasion. Tomorrow we will all get out and change trains.

Life as a whole is often compared to a journey from one station to the next. To go to Colorado Springs you go to Chicago, then Denver. To go to a Wall Street law office, you go to Par Excellence Prep, then Gothic University, then Pinstripe Law School.

Before we clamber off the train tomorrow, I would like to share some thoughts with you about the relationship of the journey we have just finished to the trip that lies beyond. What is the relationship between experience at Lawrenceville and our later lives? What has Lawrenceville meant?

First of all, I hope that it has meant mastery of basic skills in reading, writing, and arithmetic. At the same time, I hope it has also developed an awareness of the power of a mind trained in the disciplined liberal arts tradition that teaches how to put basic skills to work. I want to be quite specific about that.

Many years ago, I served for a brief time as Executive Assistant to the Governor of New Jersey. One day he called me into his office and said, "Tomorrow I will be visited by a delegation from Camden. They think we ought to dig a tunnel under the Delaware River for the second crossing in the Philadelphia area. I think we ought to build a bridge. By noon tomorrow tell me what you think we should do."

I knew nothing about bridges or tunnels but did know how to use the state library. By noon of the next day, I gave the Governor my analysis. I could do so not because I understood any of the engineering, or knew how to calculate traffic flows, land acquisition costs, Corps of Engineers' bridge requirements, or the like. What I knew was how to discover the facts that were important and organize them into a pattern that answered a specific question. The liberal arts principle is that if you have the basic skills and know how to use them, you can find out about almost anything and then apply that knowledge to a specific problem at hand.

39

Harold McMillan, when he was Prime Minister of Great Britain, reported what his Oxford don had said to him about yet another use of a liberal education. "Gentlemen," he said, "you are now about to embark upon a course of studies. . . . I would like to remind you of an important point. Some of you, when you graduate, will go on into the church, the law, politics, business, or government service. A few—I hope a very few—will become teachers. Let me make this clear to you. Except for those in the last category, teaching, nothing that you will learn in the course of your studies will be of the slightest possible use to you in after life—save only this—that if you work hard and intelligently, you should be able to detect when a man is talking rot. That, in my view, is the main if not the sole purpose of education."

A liberal arts education teaches us to discern "when a man is talking rot," and also when a man is doing something rotten. For example, in the last couple of months I have been especially interested in scapegoating, which is certainly one kind of talking and thinking rot. A friend of mine seems to know a great many people named Bozo. For example, we were watching a baseball game, and after a close call at first base my friend shouted, "You're blind, you Bozo." A little later in a political conversation, he seemed to indicate that many members of Congress came from the same family. "If it weren't for those dumb Bozos in Washington, we'd be OK." Bozos seem to suffer a wide range of afflictions. I have already mentioned the umpire who was a blind Bozo and Congressmen who are dumb. In addition, there seem to be sad Bozos, selfish Bozos, and even stinking Bozos!

A liberally educated man will, of course, recognize that Bozo talk is rot because it is an example of the simpleminded scapegoat kind of name calling that relieves us of our responsibility for accepting the complex interrelationships of our world and our own crucial involvement with all that is wrong in it, as well as with all that is right in it.

In a sense less directly related to academic instruction, how will the members of the Class of 1981 respond to their journey here? Will they be changed people, for better or for worse, because they have attended Lawrenceville? People sometimes ask me that question. They ask, "What difference will it make for someone to have been a Lawrentian?"

That's a more difficult question than the matter of what Lawrenceville has meant in terms of basic skills and the liberal arts disciplines, but it is a question that has answers.

First of all, this is a tough school. Need I tell you that? It is tough in many senses. Academic standards are high and require a lot of work if you are going to earn any degree of success. Athletic levels within the various levels of competence are demanding. You can't make the team unless you put out, whether it be House football or Varsity lacrosse. There are demanding tryouts for membership in Periwig and the Symphonic Orchestra. I hope it hasn't been all work and no play, but I know that it has been a lot more work than many high school students are willing to undertake.

Perhaps I am being too presbyterian. Especially in early June, as the rhododendron bloom on campus, this campus also conveys a sense of great beauty. I would hardly dare talk about it except in a baccalaureate address, but from time to time I have felt the sense that the beauty of this campus is not lost even on students when they are here. Just the other day, I saw a member of the Form taking photographs of some of the plantings around Foundation House. We are blessed to have lived in an environment that so smilingly speaks of beauty. If we never in any part of our journey know beauty, then we can hardly expect in any other part of our journey to want or appreciate it.

If the campus speaks to us of beauty, can it be said that the unseen human relationships speak of love? I doubt I would have used that word ten years ago, but as I grow more experienced, I think I see elements of love in almost all human affairs. The kind of loving trust that is most visible is that which is offered by a housemaster or a classroom teacher, or in a more general sense by the institution itself to each student even before he has earned it, even when he has turned his back upon that trust and deliberately violated it.

The opposite of that sort of trust is a very thick book of rules, hundreds of them, having to do with every single situation and laying forth with precision what should and should not be done and what will happen if the regulations are not scrupulously observed. Small people always want big rule books and see things in black-and-white, static terms.

The human being, however, has a divine spark within. That means you must get out of its way when it starts growing. You must give it an opportunity to be responsible, even though you know that sometimes that responsibility will be mishandled.

Perhaps this Class of 1981 can understand a little bit of what I am trying to get at. If your housemasters and teachers have trusted you, even when you have put thumbtacks on their chairs, then you have had unique opportunities to grow. In turn you will be willing to accept and trust others. Remember that, especially when you bring your own children to Lawrenceville as candidates for admission. That ought to be just after the year 2000!

You have, of course, made mistakes, but you may have learned most by making those mistakes. They weren't really all that fateful anyway except in the sense that they gave you opportunities to look into yourself in depth and learn about yourself.

Finally, I hope for you as you go through the next stages of your journey that you will carry with you some sense of the joy of sharing with others what you are doing. The kind of sharing that takes place late at night in *The Lawrence* rooms or first period of the morning when you are in a class together. At the same time, I hope you will carry with you what I have just described as the creative power of trusting others so that they can grow, and of accepting others so that they can be part of your lives.

What luggage will you then take with you as you change trains? Here's my list: basic skills, rigorous training in the liberal arts tradition, a good rot detection system, an appreciation of the joy of mastering a difficult task, an understanding of how trust encourages growth, a sense of beauty, an awareness of the importance of loving care in human relationships, and a warm feeling of having shared important relationships with others.

Gentlemen of the Graduating Class: We have made a journey together. The metaphor brings to mind other journeys: Plato's through the realms of abstract thought, Newton's through the world of physics, Christopher Columbus' to land upon the North American Continent, or Neil Armstrong's to land upon the moon. We could name a hundred others whose journeys have made a difference. All of these journeys started somewhere. I believe that you have started well and may well satisfy in your lives the deep need we all feel to make a difference with our lives. One way or another all of us make a difference: in one degree or another, and for better or for worse, as the case may be.

As a Class, you have made a difference. Though we were momentarily clattering a bit just at the end of the year, the overall record is unparalleled. You can be proud of that. I am certainly proud of you and pleased for you. It has been a happy year for me. I hope that you feel it has given to you the strengths that this great School has the power to offer you. I also hope that the year has helped you to have the sense and joy of doing something well that is difficult, of beauty as a dimension of human experience, and of the importance of trust in human relationships.

God bless the Class of 1981 and bless us all.

—From the Baccalaureate Address

PART III
The Dignity of Teaching

Saturday, November 7, 1964

This morning we welcome to the campus nearly eight hundred parents. It is our warm pleasure to share with you this day some experience of our school community. I have no illusions that a few classes attended or a brief meeting with one of my faculty colleagues will fully inform you about Lawrenceville; although, presumably you already have a considerable knowledge of Lawrenceville both from what your son says to you and from what he does *not* say.

We adults often take far too much credit in this matter of education. We accept eagerly the burden of education for our young people because we know that this is a primary obligation, but sometimes we are inclined to think of the obligation as being entirely one-sided. With loving care, we prepare pedagogical prescriptions that we diligently apply without ever having consulted with the patient about his symptoms. The process rings with moral rectitude but may also be irrelevant.

Job asks:

But where shall wisdom be found? and where is the place of understanding? Man Knoweth not the price thereof; neither is it found in the land of the living. The depth saith, it is not in me; and the sea saith, it is not with me.

These are questions that any teacher or parent must ask, and the consequent humility is the first foundation of fine teaching. The basic truth about education is that it is a central aspect of God's continuing creation. Our part is to encourage, inspire, and direct, but the vital spark of growth is the student's.

We must encourage discovery rather than *tell* mere facts. Stuffing with dates, names, vocabulary, or formulae can lead to nothing but regurgitation. I am reminded, for example, of a distinguished history teacher who was seriously concerned about the problem of teaching American history in an academic year with a fixed number of days when it was quite clear that an additional bit of American history had been added each year!

We must regard inspiration about intellectual and moral responsibility in general as more significant than spooning out any particular point of view. It is easy if one is bold, dramatic, and perhaps not particularly wise to stride like a pied piper through an academic course interpreting it and all that surrounds it in the light of one's particular prejudices and preferences. This is not teaching. Rather, it is indoctrination, and it can result only in fragile rigidity.

I hasten to add that I would not wish to be misconstrued as saying that a teacher's opinions have no place in the classroom. They do indeed have a place because conviction is an important part of the human experience, and young men must learn the meaning of conviction in the experiences and minds

45

of their elders. The expression of a conviction, however, is quite a different thing from insisting upon it and jamming it down a student's throat.

Finally, training of a young man's mind is much more than a matter of superficial discipline, although discipline may be very much involved, and discipline in the sense of *intellectual* discipline is absolutely at the heart of the educational process. I am trying to separate taskmaster drill from the more creative aspects of teaching, but I do not wish to filter out the aspects of discipline that are, in fact, important. I speak of personal responsibility, of a willingness to say "I don't know" when that is the case, and of an awareness of the meaning of detail and of thorough preparation. These are the disciplines that count.

Any class will provide ample evidence that encouragement, inspiration, and direction breed their own responses.

Indifference is the student's characteristic response to being spoon fed rather than encouraged in discovery. I well remember a certain history course that I once took under a brilliant scholar. I slept very well through most of it even though I did, in fact, have great respect for the teacher. Secondly, "spooning" runs counter to the drive for independence that characterizes the boy in school. Because he is finding his own place in the infinite dimensions of the world around him, he is infinitely independent, even to folly. Yet none can guard him; none *should* guard him. None should try to bend him into some presumably more satisfactory pattern because the conviction must ultimately be his, based on his own self-discoveries.

Petty discipline, too, has its almost automatic response. I am tempted to cite the example of my youngest son who, like most boys, hates to get out of the water when he's swimming in the summertime. There's a neat moral question involved in the decision about whether I should trick him by saying sharply, "Don't you dare get out of that water," when I know perfectly well that he will do precisely the *opposite* of what I tell him! Our young Lawrentians—your sons—are considerably older than my son, but I want you to know that it has been as much a battle for me and my faculty colleagues to get boys to the barber shop as it has been for you at home!

The truth of the matter is that education is something that grows from within each individual person. It is ultimately a question of self-discovery as a result of myriad forces and opportunities acting upon each boy. Essentially a school is not a place for sixteen-full-ounces of facts, for indoctrination, or for drillmaster routines; although each of these in a measure may have their place. Essentially, a school in the liberal arts tradition is a community rich with the opportunity for each boy to find the best in himself.

—From remarks on Parents' Day

I have been instructed by your President to speak no more than nine and seven-eighths minutes this morning. That's a difficult assignment for a Williams man otherwise given *carte blanche* at an Amherst assembly, but with due regard to your schedules—and to the football results last autumn—I shall watch my time carefully.

It's a difficult assignment anyway to speak about careers in teaching. There are many different facets of teaching and many reasons for choosing one particular age level or one particular type of institution. The most I can hope is that my remarks may raise some pertinent questions.

First of all, why teach at all? I am now too old, too overweight, and too out-of-breath to put much stock in some of the standard shibboleths. For example, one often hears about the creativity of teaching as compared with the enforced conformity of a business career, yet I observe that academic communities have their own fierce brand of conformity. In dress it is tweedy sport coats, pipes, and bow ties; in politics it's vote Democrat and go to Harvard for your Ph.D. In music it is Bach rather than Berlioz. Conversely, academic creativity is often campus-conceived as being merely intellectual, merely in skepticism, merely in detachment like Conrad's Heyst. Some of you may have read the late C. S. Lewis's science-fiction allegory *That Hideous Strength*. I commend it to you as an exploration of one community of intellectuals.

Our world is an infinitely complicated fabric involving a highly-sophisticated technology and social relationships of unprecedented subtleness. It behooves us to recognize that personal creativity, which is *prima facie* a good end that we all seek, may take a great many forms, some of them quite unexpected.

I have used a straw man to lead us to a moral issue involved in the question, "Why teach?," and on moral grounds we find no help at all. I refer explicitly, of course, to the churches and philosophies. For the most part, the church since John Calvin has been conspicuous for its vagueness in the question of careers. We in America have inherited some Calvin in the form of transmogrified Puritanism. Americans tend to believe that work—*per se*—is good and that more work is—*per se*—better. We are inclined to believe that personal success is somehow equated with personal goodness, and we further like to think, paradoxically, that service in the professions is somehow best of all because the motive is theoretically to serve others. The American vocational hero is a composite of Paul Bunyan, Oliver Wendell Holmes, and Dr. Dooley. But if there is among us this morning some embryonic Bunyan, Holmes, or Dooley, I doubt very much that his moral commitment is dominant in his thinking about a career.

The choice of a teaching career, like the choice of other vocations, rests upon the bedrock of self-knowledge. The matrices of home life, of early schooling, of interests, and of inherited and developed aptitudes shape a man's grain towards teaching. The question is not so much, "Why teach?" as it is, "Who and what am I?" How can I best commit the broadest spectrum of my characteristics and attributes?

Try some of these questions and draw the inevitable inferences:

Do you like working with others or on your own?

What are your special manual, artistic, social, or intellectual skills?

Do you prefer and admire thought or action?

Are you by nature more comfortable in routine and established circumstances or in quickly changing and doubtful situations?

Do you have a zest for risk, for the gamble, or do you feel uncomfortable when stakes are high and penalties heavy?

Is your temperament level and well-ballasted or is it mercurial: full of ups and downs?

Whom do you admire and why?

What are your honestly appraised tastes and distastes?

If your answers suggest the possibility of teaching, we can begin profitably to talk about various kinds of teaching careers.

Most of you will naturally tend to think first of all about college teaching. In our society, the professor has more status than the skull-cracker in a blackboard jungle. His hands are cleaner. Moreover, college teaching is closer to you, more real and more exciting—as it should be—than teaching at other levels.

But don't let that familiarity and excitement color your own self-analysis. Fine school men generally recognize in themselves a greater interest in and aptitude for *students* and *skills* than in restricted disciplines and scholarly publication. If you wish to make a revealing test, I suggest that you take a single issue of P.M.L.A. and read it through from beginning to end, every last desiccated word. If you can make your way through that long Sahara of serendipity to the last black period and feel that the journey has been worthwhile, college is for you.

Forgive me for a cheap trick. Some of my best friends are college teachers—their scholarship is the lifeblood of education—and there is also room in secondary schools for genuine scholarship. My Lawrenceville colleague, Dr. Thomas H. Johnson, is America's foremost authority on Amherst's Emily Dickinson, but a secondary-school man generally has somewhat less exclusively "publish-or-perish" motivation. Some have called it, incidentally, "publish *and* perish."

A secondary-school teacher's strongest motive is probably that he himself found learning exciting and sees it as a good thing to enable others to share that excitement. He also likes to continue learning himself and to associate

48

with people who share his interests and values. In a word he is constantly surprised, as one of my colleagues puts it, to find that he can earn a living by doing what he likes. He has not, however, been attracted by salaries, which at best by today's standards mean genteel poverty in spite of recent substantial improvement.

I personally feel that school teaching is almost unique in twentieth century America in offering immediate, major, and independent responsibility. To go into the classroom where total responsibility rests with the teacher is the most demanding challenge that I know. First, this responsibility is even broader in a residential school, and a residential school offers further a sense of identity in a finite community which can have a coherent philosophy. This, too, I regard as nearly unique in American life today. There's no commuting or vocational schizophrenia in residential school life.

Some may ask about public as opposed to independent or private schools. Here, too, there are in my judgment misleading shibboleths. To put it bluntly, there are many different kinds of schools: good, bad, and indifferent. To distinguish among them on the basis of their sources of income is like judging a man by the coat he wears. Would you, for example, care to conclude that Amherst is inferior to the University of Massachusetts because it is privately supported rather than tax-supported?

I can make a case that the pluralism of American education is the secret of its great vitality, and this is precisely what I do when I'm on the road seeking funds for Lawrenceville. But this philosophical view seems to me irrelevant to career choice. The important thing is fit your own interests and abilities to the teaching situation that promises to be most fruitful for you. There's a great need for fine, well-trained men at every level and in every kind of education.

Finally I want to say two very personal things. I meet every morning with an English class and seldom sit down in the classroom without thinking of Chaucer's phrase, "And gladly would he learn and gladly teach." Perhaps even more fundamentally as I ask, "Why teach,"—and I hope I will not embarrass you by so putting my heart on my sleeve—I think of Aristotle and of the great creative power of a trained intelligence. To teach is to share in creation.

—From remarks made at Amherst College

September 11, 1970

We now turn to a summer event that has touched us all closely. Frank Heyniger's death on August 24, 1970, at *The Meadows,* was a blow to our School community and takes from us untimely a man whose presence and qualities touched almost every aspect of the life of the Lawrenceville School. We shall miss him sorely as a schoolman. We shall miss him sorely also as a friend, and there could be no more appropriate time than this to say that the two are synonymous. Let us rise for one minute of silent prayer for Frank, for his family, for those he cared for, and for those who care for him.

We are all aware that there are thunder clouds around us, in the colleges and universities, in the great public-high-school systems, and in particular among many of our residential schools. That our own enrollment picture is presently favorable and that we have begun to learn some of the ways of dealing with currently negative attitudes among students should not blind us. We ourselves have had some dark clouds pass over, and an occasional shower has suggested that we are just as vulnerable as anyone else to the agonies of schools in general and to the particular problems of falling enrollment and discontent that are creating such acute problems in comparable schools.

A lot of people in schools today feel like Robert Benchley struggling to finish an article. He wrote the word "The," then he drew a blank. He looked at the paper, he cursed, he paced the floor, and finally he went out and got plastered. Then he came back and wrote, "The hell with it."

We all have a deeply personal stake in what happens in all schools in America. Just as the children in schools are our children so will our future be of their making. We had better do the very best job we can. The job that we can do focuses on one key point that seems particularly appropriate because Frank Heyniger, whose memory is so important to us, expressed that point so well in his commitment to Lawrenceville. There were all sorts of things about the life of the School that Frank loved, and he participated in them enthusiastically. He loved sports and undertook to coach soccer at my request when we had an emergency and even though he already had a very full schedule; he was a regular official at swimming meets throughout the winter months; and he was devoted to golf.

There were a lot of things Frank didn't like, however, and he made no bones about it. Because he admired the real pros, he detested amateur music, but there he would be at Glee Club Concerts on snowy February evenings. That made a key difference the next morning for the second tenor in Frank's European History class. Frank disliked amateur dramatic productions, but there he was along with Ad attending every performance of every school play. He served as Lower School-Relief Master years beyond the expectation of his tenure.

Books, syllabi, classrooms, and visual aids are important, but not crucial. Systems of residence, discipline, and counseling are important, but not crucial. Administrative procedures and flexibility are important, but not crucial. What really counts are the personal relationships that give meaning to a bare structure that can provide only a skeleton.

I believe along with Theodore Roszak, who makes the case so persuasively in *The Making of a Counter Culture,* that "The alienated young are giving shape to something that looks like the saving vision our endangered civilization requires." Given this generalization, I also agree with Roszak that there is no avoiding the need to understand and to educate the young in what they are about. They do not know, and it is up to us to make what is happening have a fruitful outcome. A dog which scratches doesn't know it has fleas. We do, and we can help.

That help must be in terms of personal relationships and personal commitments to all that is happening within the life of the School.

Herman Hesse writes in *Steppenwolf:*

"Human life is reduced to real suffering, to hell, only when two ages, two cultures and religions overlap. . . There are times when a whole generation is caught in this way between two ages, two modes of life, with the consequence that it loses all power to understand itself and has no standard, no security, no symbol acquiescence."

In a somewhat similar vein, Jerry Rubin comments in *Do It,* "The biggest social problem in the country today is loneliness." I think that Herman Hesse and Jerry Rubin are right, and I think furthermore that we have both a unique responsibility and unique opportunities precisely because of the kind of school that we are.

The questions we ought to ask ourselves as individuals go something like this:

Can we convey the conviction that we teach what we teach because it is important both to us and in larger dimensions, and not simply because it is required?

Can we demand hard work and the highest standards in the classroom, in activities, and in athletics, and at the same time bring interest and joy to each day so that it seems worthwhile to be a young person at Lawrenceville?

Can we say to a young man, "Don't be a damn fool" when it needs to be said? Can we josh him with a sense of humor into new perceptions and let those new perceptions be a measure of his growth?

Can we avoid falling back on skeletal rules, regulations, traditions, and procedures that offer only a convenient way to organize our lives, not the necessary hot, human fulcrum of action and growth?

And finally, do we know where we stand in our own minds on the crucial issues large and small: from neatness and classroom honesty to Indo-China and McLuhan's global village?

Young people do not expect adults to agree with them necessarily; what they want is straightforward discussion and some proof that adults themselves know where they stand. What they want is to be taken seriously as human beings.

Our objective at Lawrenceville is to create a place where people grow: where faculty members become ever more competent and more self-fulfilling, where boys become competent and confident young men, having enough understanding of themselves to take a useful part in a world that sorely needs intelligent and humane people.

In pursuing this objective, we must recognize that our academic program provides only a scaffolding. Our residential facilities are only a step removed from a motel, and our administrative resources are purely an arbitrary convenience rigged mostly for the benefit of the faculty.

The touchstone lies in personal relationships one with another and with the boys who are in our care. It is that understanding that Frank Heyniger's life as a schoolman and as a friend so completely expressed. A letter from an alumnus speaking of what he had learned from Frank said, "Wow, how much more we need affection than praise."

We have been wonderfully endowed in many respects, and our opportunities are manifold. We must make every effort to maximize our genuine personal involvement with the life of the School as we take our part in the creative process that lies at the heart of the great profession of teaching.

—From remarks to the Faculty at the Head Master's Dinner

May 28, 1975

Twenty-five years ago, Mary Elizabeth and I arrived at Lawrenceville in late August. The process of moving on a dreadfully hot and humid day had rubbed our nerves raw, and, to use a euphemism, we were somewhat "surprised" about the housing to which we had been assigned. In short, that August afternoon was something of a low spot.

Around the corner came a cheerful, bright-eyed man who said, "Oh, you must be the McClellans. I've been expecting you, and I'm here to help. I've been at Lawrenceville twenty-one years myself, and it's been a great place for me. You'll feel just the same way when you have your twenty-five year dinner."

The speaker was, of course, Pat Coughlan, and he restored our souls on the spot. There have been ups and downs since, but I share Pat's conviction that Lawrenceville is a fine place to be, though I certainly wasn't thinking about a twenty-five year dinner on that hot summer day. For twenty-four years I've thought of that event as something that happens to other people!

This evening I think especially of other people because memories bob to the surface of my mind in a quite random manner. What about those nicknames? Next to me sits the Hummingbird. Two Tiller Tom is on my right. The Easter Bunny. Who knows Chrome Dome? Who can identify Carbon Lung? Wasn't Black Jack the greatest? How about Steady Teddy? And Frank Heyniger's fund of stories; I never heard him tell the same one twice.

Part of my thinking tonight is about people who have been important to me and to Lawrenceville during the years of gradually moving up the seniority list in the catalogue from the bottom to rank number six on the active list.

In my first letter to the faculty following my appointment as Head Master, I spoke of my pride in the Lawrenceville practice—unique in America—of writing the title of Head Master as two separate words. I have never felt that a Head Master should be other than a faculty member entrusted with special responsibilities. My first professional claim is to the title "teacher." I do not wish to be engulfed in what Pung Wright used to call so appropriately "That great abstraction, the Administration."

So it is that I speak this evening principally as a teacher, and my first thought is that I am proud especially of the quality of my colleagues. I will hardly risk offending anyone if I say that I think we assembled here are a remarkably fine group of men and women devoted to the profession of teaching.

Teaching is the best—if not necessarily the oldest—profession. It does not, however, meet contemporary American criteria for the good life: creamy Cadillacs, green Country Clubs, oodles of possessions, and bunnied jet planes.

Teaching is the best profession, perhaps, because as a housemaster said to me just the other day, "We all want to do good with our lives." That's something quite different from the status consumption of commercial America.

Doing good with our lives requires accepting the burdens of becoming

53

genuinely involved with other human beings. For teachers that means the young who are the future. The catch is that each rose of high principle has its corresponding thorn, capable of wounding us:

To care is to experience anxiety.

To make a commitment is to know failure.

To have purpose is to suffer frustration.

To try to accomplish something specific is to make a mistake.

To have high ideals is to wrestle with disillusionment.

To have hope is to feel despair.

Doing good with our lives as teachers means that we accept burdens. Otherwise we might just as well go to Florida, sink into the warm sands, and vegetate like comfortable carrots.

The good life of the teacher is burdensome precisely because it involves caring, commitment, purpose, goals, ideals, and hope. These truths are self-evident, and we all know them when we stop to think about them, though sometimes the thorns seem more evident than the blooms. These truths are also borne more easily when they are shared more fully.

When Lawrenceville was refounded in the late nineteenth century, the governing phrase in John C. Green's will read that his trustees were to use his legacy "for such purposes of friendship" as they might determine. That phrase would not pass muster with the Internal Revenue Service today, but it seems especially appropriate this evening.

The art of the classroom and the House is essentially an art that must be practiced alone. We as individual teachers and housemasters must accept the awful responsibility of being part of creation. That would be an individually overwhelming obligation if we had not also a sense of sharing with each other.

This evening's celebration—like those that have gone before it, like those that will follow—expresses our support for each other in one of man's most difficult responsibilities.

I stand before you, somewhat wounded, mostly bald, much moved by this experience, and devoted to teaching as a profession.

—From remarks made at the Faculty Dinner

May 28, 1985

About two weeks ago, someone from Morristown Beard phoned to ask me what the title of my remarks this evening would be. The question was just a little embarrassing because I had not prepared my remarks even though I knew exactly what I wanted to say.

At any rate, I had no difficulty in deciding about my title: "And gladly learn." That seemed to me especially appropriate for an occasion recognizing the academic achievements of the best students in this fine school. "And gladly learn."

How many of you, I wonder, recognize the quote? It comes from the *Prologue* to Chaucer's *Canterbury Tales*. And there are two parts to the quote, which is part of the description of the Clerk from Oxford. The first is, "and gladly would he learn." The second is, "and gladly teach." In the company of those who have learned so well, it seems appropriate to speak about those who teach.

Teaching as a career is not popular today. In fact, we Americans have never thought particularly well of those who teach. We like people who open up frontiers, who build skyscrapers, who sail ships around the world, who accumulate vast fortunes, and who wield visible political power.

My father-in-law expressed it well when he said shortly after he learned that I intended to be a teacher, "Well, Bruce, I guess that's all right if you want to be a teacher. I just want you to know that I think you could make a success of it in the real world."

In my view, teaching is "the real world" in a sense far more significant than any other career. Teachers transmit civilization from one generation to the next, and I can think of no responsibility more important.

A good many years ago, Sir James George Frazer in *The Golden Bough* wrote a significant chapter titled "Our Debt to the Savage." What he said was that every advance made in human understanding has been earned by some previous generation. The triumph of space flight, for example, rests upon hundreds of thousands of small understandings of the physical world that have been accumulated throughout the centuries of human experience. To use Frazer's own language, "we stand on the shoulders of those who have gone before us." It is the teacher who conveys those accumulated understandings to the student, who in turn makes new discoveries and discovers new horizons.

Crucial though teaching may be, one would never know it from contemporary attitudes. Not long ago, Ernest Boyer, former U.S. Commissioner of Education and now President of the Carnegie Foundation for the Advancement of Teaching, said, "In a thousand separate ways we tell our students that teaching in schools is not a dignified profession." So it is that teachers may not teach so gladly as did the Clerk of Oxford. So it is that the best of students often steer clear of teaching.

The sad result is—as one person has observed—that "teaching is the most depressed profession in the United States." Denigration of teaching is pervasive. No less a person than W. H. Auden observed not so long ago that, "a schoolmaster was the last person he would like to sit next to at a dinner party."

I would love to argue with Auden on that point. Many years ago, I was discussing with a colleague why we enjoyed teaching. He observed, "I like to teach because I like the people who like to teach." The longer I have myself been teaching the more I think that answer makes a lot of sense. I like the people who like to teach, and I love to have them at my dinner parties, as compared for example with automobile salesmen, accountants, Hollywood producers, or millionaires. Mr. Auden, I would love to have taken you to task. Perhaps some poets aren't particularly good dinner companions either!

Bart Giamatti, the retiring President of Yale University, put it very simply when he said, "A liberal education is at the heart of a civil society, and at the heart of a liberal education is the act of teaching."

Fred Borsch, Dean of the Chapel at Princeton University, places teaching in an even broader perspective. He writes:

> *"A concern for teaching is as old as thoughtful education. 'If you ask what is the good of education,' Plato wrote, 'The answer is easy: that education makes good men and that good men act nobly.' Whether or not the answer is easy, it was certainly taken as axiomatic until this century that a chief purpose, if not the chief purpose, of education is to benefit society and the individual by enabling its recipients to become good and to act nobly."*

As you will gather, I believe that teaching is the greatest of professions. What's more, I think it's appropriate to address the matter of teaching on an occasion that honors those who have been superb students. There is all too much evidence that Mark Twain's observations about teachers is more widely accepted today than it has ever been. You will remember that Twain said, "those who can't, teach."

I am myself coming to the conclusion of my classroom career. Being a teacher has meant much to me, and I am particularly dismayed that teaching should be a profession held in such low regard in our country. The consequences can ultimately only be catastrophic.

As I believe that teaching is crucial to a democratic society and to the quality of our civilization, so I believe that teaching can be deeply satisfying to each of us as individuals. It is my conviction that most of us yearn deeply for immortality. I can think of no form of immortality greater than having had an impact on the life of a young person growing up. I cannot calculate how many students have been in classes with me. What I do know is that each of them is in some way different because of the time we have spent together.

In some ways the awareness that I have somehow made a difference to all of those students is frightening. I cannot help but wonder whom I have damaged or whom I have not helped to realize his full potential. At the same time, I know that I have also given new horizons, new life to many others. Not long ago a student wrote in a paper that he was fearful of accepting "the risk that we take in caring for others." That is indeed a great risk, yet it is a risk that I believe is well worth taking.

Great teaching, observes Roland Oliver, requires "the alertness of a lion tamer, the polish of a great actor, and the tremendous communication of energy which alone can convey truth."

Dangerous as it is, a teaching career is satisfying because it resonates to the deepest pulses of human growth. There is nothing easy about it at all. Nor is it in any sense a sheltered occupation. Quite to the contrary, it is on the front lines of human experience. Those who gladly learn perhaps have had some sense of the significance of a teacher's career. Those who have gladly learned perhaps also have some sense that they may gladly teach.

These are very personal remarks that spring from a growing and deep conviction about my own career as a teacher. I trust that what you have achieved here you will put to good use and not just strive to make money or to acquire power. Whatever your occupation may be, I hope that you will always value teachers and teaching. I suppose I shall have to be honest in closing and say that I hope also some of *you* will become teachers.

—*From remarks at the* Cum Laude *Dinner, Morristown Beard School*

September 28, 1987

In the autumn of 1939—almost fifty years ago—I arrived at Deerfield as a student. Since then, I have been a member of the faculty, a trustee of what is now "Historic Deerfield," and a good friend of three Deerfield Head Masters and many faculty members as well as of a number of fellow alumni. These associations have been important to me, and I am grateful for them as well as proud of them. I am grateful and proud particularly today as the recipient of the Heritage Award in the School's 190th year.

In the early nineteenth century, a minor English poet wrote some lines that I happened across last week as I began to think about what I might say here this morning. "If there were dreams to sell," he asked, "what would you buy?" If memory serves me well, Deerfield years are a time of dreams. A lifetime lies ahead, and anything is possible. If there were dreams to sell, what would *you* buy?

That's another way of thinking about what we value most. Have you ever dreamed, for example, about being a king? Some of you may remember the conversation about kings and dukes and earls as Huck Finn and Jim floated on their raft down the big river:

"How much do a king git?" asks Jim.
"Get?" says Huck, "Why, they get a thousand dollars a month if they want it; they can have just as much as they want; everything belongs to them."

A little later, Huck explains what a harem is and guesses that King Solomon had about a million wives. Jim says he'd forgotten about that and continues, "A harem's a bod'n house, I reck'n. Mos' likely dey has rackety times in de nussery. En I reck'n de wives quarrels considable." Jim's common sense tells him that even at a thousand dollars a month and with a million wives in a harem, a king might find himself living in something less than a dreamworld.

What dream will you buy? As I asked myself that question, the picture that unexpectedly materialized was of a fur-lined tea cup. You may know the one I mean. Salvador Dali painted it along with a limp watch and lots of other surrealistic things. I take the fur-lined cup as the ultimate symbol of a western culture gone mad with consumerism.

Not long ago, my wife and I were trying to decide what to do about the blizzard of Christmas mail-order catalogues that is just beginning. We believe in recycling, so we didn't want to take them to the dump. Where could we put them until we could take them to a recycling center? We finally settled on an unused chest just about big enough for a well-fed St. Bernard dog to sleep in comfortably. It may be large enough to store all those catalogues, but I'm a bit skeptical about that.

I'm even more skeptical about a society that frames its dreams so largely in terms of essentially useless things. It could be quite comical to cull from those Christmas catalogues a list of the consumer absurdities, but it would also be tragically sad because, by far, the largest part of the world's population remains chronically diseased, hungry, and fearful.

Well then, perhaps we ought to think twice about a dream of living like Huck Finn's king on a thousand dollars a month with a million wives in the harem. Perhaps we ought to think twice about a dream of getting ahead in the consumer race that advertisers so aggressively urge upon us. After all, how many furlined tea cups can you use?

Let's look at this question of our dreams from another point of view. I believe that above all other things we humans dream of being immortal. Over eons of time, mankind has responded to that felt need in many ways. As parents, men and women live on through the children whom they bear, nourish, support, and finally set free. As teachers, adults transmit civilization from one generation to the next and thereby live on. To be part of creation as a parent or as a teacher is, in my judgment, a privilege without parallel.

So there it is. I urge you to dream about teaching as a career. There's not much money in it. You don't live like Huck's king, and you are almost by definition on the fringes of our consumer society. In fact, a teacher may feel like a Russian dissident in Moscow if he by some chance winds up in Hollywood, Palm Beach, or Park Avenue. He may even feel like that sometimes in Deerfield or Lawrenceville.

It's not easy to think about teaching as a career in our society. My father-in-law thought of teachers as people who couldn't compete in the savage environment of the business jungle. He would not have understood Shelley's dictum that "poets are the unacknowledged legislators of the world." By way of perspective, I might report that my brother-in-law taught for ten years at one of Britain's most distinguished "public" schools and then moved to this country to become a wildly successful entrepreneur. It is his considered judgment that anyone who can survive five years in a classroom can run circles around any banker or businessman.

Quite aside from my in-laws, I want to share with you this morning my conviction that there are many different ways to serve our society usefully. We need doctors, lawyers, merchant chiefs, automobile salesmen, manufacturers, farmers, poets, and a host of others. What we do not need is people who dream chiefly in terms of money and possessions.

Especially I urge the deep satisfaction of teaching: probably the least-valued and most-endangered career path in America today. You probably know the statistics and the facts. Objective test scores of teachers in training have steadily declined as other career opportunities have opened up for those intelligent, patient, and able women who were for so long the heart and soul of our elementary and secondary schools. In literacy, mathematical skills, the sciences, and languages we are steadily falling behind others. The demographics of the next decade indicate clearly that we shall be losing a desperately large segment of our skilled teachers just as a new bulge of students will be entering school.

In his opening convocation address, my successor at Lawrenceville spoke of his faculty colleagues as "men and women who live what they teach, and who teach not for fame, or money, or power, but simply because it is worthwhile." It is a career very much worth dreaming about.

I say that partly because it is exactly what I feel at the conclusion of thirty-seven years of teaching. If you want to exercise major and important responsibility early in your career, try the classroom. If you want to have fun and stay fit, try coaching. If you want to walk to work rather than fight the freeways or suffer on commuter trains, try a residential school. If you would like to be involved in an enterprise where different age levels participate on an equal footing, think of being a faculty member. If you would like to be creative but aren't Picasso, try the blackboard. Teaching is an art, not a science. Though it doesn't happen all the time or every day, I have felt in the classroom more often than not the enriching sense of being part of ongoing creation. What more can you dream of?

Here in this memorable place, many Deerfield teachers became importantly a part of my life. They helped to create what I am. I think of Bart Boyden's demanding rigor about punctuation; of Dick Hatch opening up Shakespeare to me; of Russ Miller's current history briefings; of Mrs. Boyden's bringing molecular structure magnificently to life. The list could go on—and probably should go on,—but I forbear because many of those whom I might mention have gone on to that great classroom where there is no chalk dust, and others no longer live in Deerfield.

The summer issue of the *Alumni Magazine* carries an article titled "Remembering Red" about Red Sullivan, one of the most memorable faculty members of his era. The author closes with a sentence that sums up what I believe is the bedrock truth about a career in teaching. "[Red] knew that what he had done was worth the life he gave it."

There's a dream for you to have a dream about.

—From the Deerfield Heritage Award Acceptance Speech

PART IV
The Divinity of Children

This morning we welcome nearly eight hundred parents to the campus. This is a special occasion for us because it provides an opportunity to share with each parent some of the meaning of the Lawrenceville experience: on the athletic field, in a classroom, and here, in chapel.

We are conscious of our debt to you who have given us your sons. We know that you will enjoy sharing with us some of the excitement that we find in working with your children as they grow to manhood in many different ways.

The central fact about teaching is that it is a form of creation. Each child has infinite possibilities for growth. Each boy is an individual who must ultimately stand upon his own two feet. If parents and teachers do their jobs well, there will emerge from the soft clay of adolescence a young man of independence, integrity, competence, and self-confidence.

My generalizations have so far been impeccable. Ralph Waldo Emerson said much the same thing in his essay "Self-Reliance." More recently, David Riesman has made a best-seller out of an extremely dull book by calling it *The Lonely Crowd.* Riesman's phrases "inner-directed" and "other-directed" have become part of contemporary folklore.

We all believe in the infinite worth of individuals and in the creative role of parents and teachers. We all believe in self-reliance and sturdy self-confidence for our sons. When we get down to brass tacks, however, are we always willing to accept the consequences of these convictions? Are we willing to accept the consequences of our conviction that every boy now in school is different from every other boy? The consequences of our conviction that every boy has capacities for growth far beyond our comprehension?

These are questions that I pose rhetorically, not to belittle parents, who hear entirely too much belittling anyway; rather I wish to affirm a touchstone for the whole Lawrenceville community.

We believe in boys. We believe in your sons. Again my generalizations are impeccable, and you could hardly imagine anything more diplomatic for me to say. Let me point briefly, however, to some of the consequences that flow from our belief in your sons.

One corollary of this conviction is that we understand the School to be something quite different from a social-stamping machine designed to turn out a product standardized in manners, dress, and language. Such machines are easy to engineer. If that were our objective, we could, with relative ease, turn out identical and recognizable production-line models in our graduation classes each year. We believe in your sons too much, however, to think that we have the right or the authority to impress upon them some preconceived mold of our own making.

Instead, we hope that each boy has an opportunity to discover himself as he becomes himself. The shape bursts outwards from within. This is the fact that we respect profoundly. The shape bursts outwards from within.

A second corollary is very similar. We have too much respect for your sons to think that we as teachers are mere stuffers and sealers of envelopes.

Teaching is something much more than telling or filling up the student with the right ingredients in the right proportions. Facts, techniques, and ideas he must have, but having them, he is not necessarily educated.

Thirdly, we believe too much in your sons to wrap them up in some sort of superficial moral and ethical packaging. There is no way to provide attitudes guaranteed to be bland and conventional except at the price of destroying the individual. If you think that we teachers are never in conflict with your sons, you underestimate us both. If you expect us to condition your son to accept you in all things, you do not understand how deeply we are committed to him.

Education is the voyage of self-discovery on which every human being must take passage alone. In every class from Greek, to Physics, to History, the ultimate subject is the student. The best teacher liberates. He liberates what lies within the student and avoids the perilous temptations to affix some social grace, some particular skill, or some shallow moral view.

The best teacher, coach, or Housemaster knows that boys must be trusted if they are to become all the things we want them to be. Knowing full well that there will be mistakes large and small, sometimes even catastrophes, he must still trust them because he believes in them, because he knows that this is the only way they can learn as individuals to stand on their own two feet.

Independence, integrity, competence, and self-confidence: these are the qualities we seek. None can be imposed from the outside. All must be generated from within.

There is a considerable body of thought today that would deny my thesis this morning. A man would be better off, it is said, if he were fitted more carefully to live with his neighbor. Men would be happier, it is said, if they were machine-adjusted to a particular place in society. After all, isn't it absurd that when we go shopping for a sport coat we have to look at short, medium, and long sizes in each measurement? Why not breed the race to three or four standard sizes and let it go at that?

This is a view that I categorically reject and that is diametrically opposed to our convictions about what we are trying to do here at Lawrenceville. We believe in your sons and offer them our trust. Only through that trust on the part of parents as well as teachers can they become educated and worthwhile human beings.

—From remarks made on Parents' Day

November 4, 1972

We take pleasure in sharing this day with parents of the boys whom we teach and with whom we live. You have given us your sons in trust, and we take that trust seriously. We regard it as the greatest of opportunities to share in the future of our country and to share, in an even larger sense, in the very process of creation itself. No man or woman could ask for more.

Because we are part of creation—always ongoing, always changing, always new—we constantly find our best-laid plans going awry. We constantly need to examine what we are doing. We constantly must respond to situations that do not have a recognizable precedent.

In several different ways it is easier for a teacher to live with boys growing to manhood than it is for the boy's own parents. For one thing, we are not quite so emotionally involved, though neither can we allow ourselves to be disengaged in a process that necessarily requires emotional involvement. For another, we have a broader sample to work with, so that we can begin to see patterns not so evident within individual family units. Uniquely among enterprises in American society, schools tend to sustain conversation and dialogue between age levels. There is not as much chronological—or perhaps I should say gerontological—stratification in schools as there is in the world away from the campus. To put it another way, in the course of my usual responsibilities I may be talking with everyone from a thirteen-year-old First Former to a forty-year teaching veteran in the space of just a few minutes. The same would be true for everyone else within this School community.

Speaking of that First Former, I am reminded of a story that I have told on several different occasions this autumn. One Sunday afternoon, just at the beginning of the school year, I encountered a bright-eyed boy and said to him, "What have you been doing today?"

"Oh, I took a long walk," he answered.

"Well," I said, "What did you see?"

"Well, I don't know just what I saw. As a matter of fact, I was on a part of the campus that I had never seen, and I was lost. Things had changed all around."

I have used the story to introduce the topic of change at Lawrenceville, and certainly there have been visible changes in recent years. For one thing, the social changes of American culture have had their impact on campus in many ways, some obvious, some not so clear. At the same time, this particular school year has begun with a series of changes in living patterns that are more radical than any since the refounding and rebuilding of the School in the late nineteenth century.

Changes are always unsettling, and in the narrowest and most intimate sense, the awareness that one's own child changes in the process of growing up is by definition unsettling to parents. Not so long ago, I talked with some parents about their son. They were concerned that he did not seem to communicate with them as he had in the past. They were concerned as well that he did not seem to take their word (about a particular situation) as the gospel truth.

I used then a poor image, of a kind I too often employ, and the more I thought about the image, the more it seemed relevant to our gathering here. I compared the boy to a rocket shooting towards the moon. The energy thunders, the guidance system spins, the engines ignite as the rocket pulsates between supporting structures, and then all of a sudden, away it goes through a zone of turbulence and poor radio communication to emerge in soaring stratospheric flight.

The image is corny, and I am not at all proud of it. It does, however, touch upon several significant aspects of young men growing up today.

First of all, it should not surprise any parent of an older adolescent boy that somehow communications are becoming garbled. There is a "zone of silence" through which the young person passes as he seeks to reach out to his own peers and to establish relationships with other adults and other life-styles than those with whom and with which he is most familiar. Many years ago, a wise headmaster said to me: "You must always remember that for most boys life in a residential school is the first experience they have on their own." This world is especially theirs. They must make their own way. It does not matter who their parents are, where they live, or what trappings of background may be available. In a residential school community the great opportunity is for the boy to be on his own within parameters that guard him against seriously endangering himself but that also allow him to try out his own unique forms of self-expression. That is the great opportunity of the residential school.

Let's look at that rocket again. Just as there are structures that support the vehicle and release it only when it seems to be well started, so there are cultural patterns of nation, region, school, and family that provide support during the initial period of a young person's growth. Those supporting structures have changed vastly within the last five years, and I do not think I need to expatiate on that point this morning. There was a time when a Brooks Brothers coat and a regimental tie served as adequate structure for a boy's self-respect and ambition. There was a time when an Anglo-Saxon name carried with it implications of place, acceptance, and prosperity. There was a time when color of skin inevitably provided structure: sometimes easy and complacent, sometimes negative and disturbing.

On this morning, I might well be construed as a high prophet of traditional structures, but I am convinced that in challenging those structures, America has entered upon a new era with great promise for the future. As in all periods of change, there are hazards that we must accept. In particular, we find it difficult to accept the change with regard to our own children. We do not want them to be put in difficult positions, or to make hard choices, or to be in positions of risk. We yearn to protect them. There can be no doubt that in America prior to 1967 this School, and much that it represented provided a convenient and easy channel for boys to grow up in. A channel in which we all had confidence.

For myself, however, I find that even though that guidance structure has changed so radically and, in fact, has made growing up more difficult for many of us, the long-range benefits far outweigh the present discomfort. We were in those years past—in a very real sense—boys becoming bigger boys. Now, I think, there is a good chance that boys can become men. Girls may become women. In short, I believe that America can reach a kind of maturity that it has rarely experienced in the past.

By maturity, I mean a willingness to accept creative diversity within the unity of a common understanding. There we are with that word creative again. And again, I think of my very bad image: that rocket ship headed out towards space.

Perhaps the missile is not, after all, a poor analogy, not as poor as some that I have used on occasions!

A young man arriving today at adulthood has before him a whole new universe to explore both literally and figuratively, both geographically and internally. Dickens must have felt something similar about the London that he knew when he began one of his novels, "It was the best of times; it was the worst of times." As I quote from Dickens, I know also that I am saying what men always have said about their times and about their children. That is the glory of life. That is the glory of teaching. It also expresses the terror and the paradox.

If you have no other response to your visit with your sons today and to this campus, I would hope that you might feel that we are part of this country, not just a backwater of special privilege, not just a preserve from the past, not just a place through which one walks to see how life once was.

Rather I would hope that you have a sense of present concern, present understanding, and forward commitment.

—From remarks made on Parents' Day

November 2, 1974

This is an extraordinarily beautiful, New Jersey November day, and we have had unusually fine weather through the autumn. That's always good for the beginning of the school year. But looking to a larger scheme of things, I am much concerned about the storm clouds all around us and have shared my concern already with the Trustees, with the faculty, and with the students. The oil cartel, the world-wide shortage of food, and an apparent inability on the part of our political leadership to respond vigorously to the problems we face, all suggest that we are in for a difficult time. Whether we shall have brief showers or a major storm no one can yet say.

Lawrenceville today is in a strong position. The Trustees' stewardship of the School's resources has been good. Support from alumni, parents, and friends continues in spite of the dubious economic picture. Personal commitment on the part of all of the elements of the Lawrenceville community is, if anything, stronger now than it has been in the past.

There is no question in my mind, however, but that we must batten down the hatches. Simple prudence requires that we conserve our resources—conserve them in every sense—and focus as precisely as possible upon our central purpose of educating young men. At the same time, we must be careful in the process of conserving resources not to lose our momentum. In the process of battening down the hatches, we don't want to suffocate the crew.

So it is that almost every turning point we reach during the current year will be made in the context of what is happening in the whole world. We will be acutely in the mainstream of history. This observation applies to each of us in all of our lives as well as to Lawrenceville in particular. History too often seems to be something that happened—in the past tense—to someone else. It is all too evident for Americans today that history is now.

The task at hand is the task of history. That's always been true, but perhaps it is more evident now than in the last quarter-century of American life. We have been insulated from that truth for too long because of our great wealth of natural resources, given to us without our having earned them, and finite in the last analysis, though we have not realized that fact.

Here, on the Lawrenceville campus, being part of history means a student staying up late to put finishing touches on a top-quality essay for English; rehearsing again and again for a brilliant piano concert; sharing a team's defeat with courage, or its victory with humility.

High performance, high standards, and broad moral responsibility are what Lawrenceville ideally is all about. But let's for a moment be iconoclasts and ask why that should be. Why impose such burdens on the young in a world that seems to impose very few real burdens on anyone? Where anything goes, isn't everything soon gone anyway? So why worry?

Our society often mocks such standards, because self-indulgent Americans have lived too long in the amazing freedom of opulent affluence. That's a truth that our leaders seem slow to grasp, even though it now appears the truth may grasp them. I believe that the country—in the sense of the

68

mainstream of American opinion—is way ahead of the politicians in this regard.

Though I equate history as it is happening around us with history as it is made by each boy in every decision, I would also hold that there is a major difference for the young person growing up. The young person must, first of all, set his own inner gyroscope spinning firmly. C. S. Lewis in *That Hideous Strength* describes the process of growing to full adulthood:

"From now onwards till the moment of final decision should meet him, the different man in him appeared with startling rapidity, and each seemed very complete while it lasted. Thus, skidding violently from one side to the other, his youth approached the moment at which he would be a person."

"His youth approached the moment at which he would be a person." That's what is happening among Lawrentians with every decision and at every moment. Young people are becoming persons. To what will he say, "Yes." To what will he say, "No." When will he hang back and say, "Maybe?" Will he reach out to seek help? Reach out to help someone else? Will he be honest with himself, about himself? Will he laugh? Not long ago, at the landing in the Dining Center, I encountered five or six Second Formers who were grinning from ear to ear and reported that they had just completed the slide on the banister from the top to the bottom of the stairs in one and a half seconds. I frowned in a Head-Masterly way and was promptly disarmed by the comment, "It's fun being an immature Lower Schooler." Of course, it is.

A commentator writing about William Butler Yeats said that he had a philosophy based on "the instinctive life of the soul and the passionate life of the body as against such destructive things as cold character and sterile knowledge that generalize all spontaneous life away to abstractions." With storm clouds looming so threateningly around us, and with an awareness that the lush pastures of the last two decades can no longer support us, we must surely as Americans think of each act as part of a larger scheme, as part of history. At the same time, we must remember in our responsibility for the nurture of young people that they are young. When all is said and done, the Yeats critic is right. The instinctive life of the soul and the passionate life of the body offer greater truths than the rigidities of cold character manipulation and the vacuity of piling packages of knowledge on top of packages of more knowledge.

There is risk in accepting the broadest parameters of growth for young people in a world that is bound to take itself more and more seriously. William Blake wrote "the road of excess leads to the palace of wisdom" for "you never know what is enough unless you know what is more than enough." That's a dangerous truth but also an important one for adults who tend to forget just how frequently they have learned from their own excesses.

On this subject of the risk involved in the education of young people, I think of Lord Chesterfield's comment to Dr. Johnson that the organized church is only willing to throw a rope to someone already standing on dry land. Adults and their institutions have to take risky chances, must throw ropes to people who are completely at sea.

The adolescent is still very much at sea: trying out roles, skidding from side to side. It is a risky business to throw a rope to him. Sometimes there are catastrophes. The only way to avoid that risk is to repress the growing young person grievously so that he is stunted, or to ignore just how much at sea the young person really is.

When all is said and done, competence alone can bestow genuine freedom and self-confidence. That is why the experience of success in one thing— Greek or *The Lawrence,* student government or Asian history, physics or Radio Station WLVL—is equal to competence, and that is the touchtone to freedom and self-knowledge. Success in one thing leads to achievement in other things. Only self-knowledge can lead to honor. None of us can live in Potemkin villages of artificial self-deceit and hope to understand what personal honor is all about. We've got to make mistakes and accept them.

That's why history is in every choice for each of the young men you have given us. History lies also in every response we make. There can be no set pattern, no easy formulae. Rather there is a continuing process of creation— always new, always growing—as we seek to create experiences that lead to competence and in turn freedom, which lead to self-knowledge and in turn honor.

—From remarks made on Parents' Day

November 8, 1975

I choose this morning to speak in an area particularly appropriate to Edith Memorial Chapel, a building long central to the life of the School but more recently fallen into the shadow of general disinterest cast by the skeptical materialism of American society.

Why do we meet in a chapel at all? After all, the Arts Center has more comfortable accommodations. To some, this building represents a decadent and outmoded gesture towards an orthodoxy of the past. The building may, perhaps, even seem offensive to some of our most devout families just as it appears indifferent to others, and we do indeed have to be honest about our attitudes. An impartial observer from Mars would, I think, find it difficult to determine just why it is that we call our world Christian.

My purpose this morning is not, however, to argue about that. What I have in mind is to explore a very simple idea that occurred to me here in chapel last Sunday morning. As part of the Service, we read a selection from the Nineteenth Psalm:

The law of the Lord is perfect, converting the soul.
The testimony of the Lord is sure, making wise the simple.
The statutes of the Lord are right, rejoicing the heart.
The commandment of the Lord is sure, enlightening the eyes.

Reading those lines, I reflected that we are living in, and your sons are growing up in, a world that too seldom says that some things are incontrovertibly wrong and others are undoubtedly right.

I am well aware of the great danger of oversimplifying. On the other hand, I am just as aware that when trust is relative and values wholly pragmatic, neither trust, nor values, can hold much meaning to young people growing up. To put it in another way, when anything goes, everything is soon gone.

Some things are right; some are wrong. A principled understanding of the choices we make is as essential to a worthwhile life as an understanding of gravity is essential to the navigation of space ships. Adults do not expect the young to have a full and firm grasp of principle. On the other hand, it is quite clear, as a distinguished observer has recently remarked, that "the culture of youth in our affluent and overconsuming society tends to be a restless, seething, and occasionally explosive mixture of fads, fancies, and self-justifications. It has too few ties to reality."

Principles are one name for ties to reality. What are those principles and where may they be found? I believe they are closer at hand and more evident than many of us—adult and young person alike—often realize. For example, history provides ample evidence of the consequences, both good and bad, that over a span of thousands of years have inevitably followed from particular choices. The Christian insight expressed in the passage from the Nineteenth Psalm is only one of many different forms allowing man to distill and express unavoidable truths about the nature of mankind. The great literature of the world teaches similarly. *Oedipus Rex, Macbeth,* and *Dr. Zhivago* teach us about the world in macrocosm as well as in microcosm, if only we have the wit to learn. In a more general sense, accumulated experience of adulthood is what parents and teachers offer the young.

Only an offer, of course. The young cannot learn simply from being told. They must make their own world and must learn from their own experiences. That is ever the glory of youth, and ever also the tribulation. We cannot save the young from themselves. Shaw remarked, "Youth is too glorious to be wasted upon the young." At the same time, I think, we ought to ask ourselves whether we help the process of learning, or hurt it, when we are reluctant to say that some things are right; some wrong.

Schools and colleges are sometimes unwilling to make judgments on principle. I cite, for example, a university that offers credit for a course in Judicial Astrology. As reported, this course is not about astrology as a historical phenomenon with cultural significance, but as a "science," and its scientific pretensions are unchallenged by the annihilating refutations received over the centuries. Or another university mentioned in the same report, in a glorious burst of ecumenicism, appoints a voodoo priest in residence. Some things are plainly wrong.

Some things are plainly right. For a school, fundamental reading and writing skills are clearly good. So also are the number skills, not because of their marketability, but because they represent a development of human ability infinitely more significant than the skill of throwing spectacular passes for the New York Jets. Any respectable school is a place where the student can learn to develop his potential to its highest level. To do that, one must begin at the beginning. It is clearly a bad choice to try to begin at the end.

As a residential school, Lawrenceville concerns itself uniquely with social principles. We cannot think that Mr. Nixon's crime was in getting caught, anymore than we can think that being discreet about rule breaking is virtuous. Put positively, it is a good thing to commit oneself to other people or to one's own ideals. That's the way we all define ourselves; that's the way we all grow.

There are plenty of guidelines to individual principles. The most famous, and perhaps the least observed, are the Ten Commandments. In a way, those Commandments are simplistic. They allow mere rule keeping to take the place of thinking of another person. Whatever the label, whatever the point of reference, there can be no doubt of the general propositions that we are less than we should be, that each of us is in need of others, that others are in need of each of us, and that growth takes place only where trust has been extended before it has been earned.

Few parents gathered in this chapel this morning would disagree with what I have been saying. How many of us would turn those same principles fully to our own lives? Ay, there's the rub.

Just the other day, I talked with a boy whom I had asked to leave school because he had twice violated dismissal regulations. In this case, he had smoked "pot" in his room at the end of an afternoon. He said to me, "I had finished my work and was just doing what my father does when he comes home at the end of the day and has a martini." That kind of reference to adult life occurs again and again among the young. It has different versions. For example, from student conversations: "Why trust others when the trusting people are wounded and powerless?" "I don't have to slave at my desk because my father knows a Trustee of Bigmoney University."

The choices we make shape our own lives and shape our children's lives as well. As the growing young person makes choices, he moves into adulthood. As sculpture emerges under the skilled hands of the artist from the mute, gray block of granite, so youth changes first in general shapes and outlines, then in the relationships of shapes with one another, and finally in details.

The analogy holds because there are principles at work as the artist creates. He must consider the quality of the stone, the kinds of instruments available to him, and the disciplines of skill that he has learned through long years of training. Only if he follows the principles in which he believes will his vision ultimately come to fulfillment.

The analogy fails, however, in another sense. The process of growing from youth to adulthood is never complete. It continues for a lifetime, and the material is infinitely complex, absolutely unique, and entirely irreplaceable. At the same time, the chief agent of creation is the individual himself. We who are participants can only provide example, encouragement, and advice when it is sought.

Parents and teachers share alike an awesome sense of the divine nature of creation. When we say divine, we express a conviction that there are principles that govern creation. If we fail to live by those principles, we short change our own sense of purpose and short change as well those whom we nurture.

The process is divine; the principles are clear. The applications are difficult. The struggle is crucial, as it has been and will be always.

I have spoken no easy truth this morning. My fear is that it will seem so. We all try hard, and we often make mistakes. But if we see that what we are doing in nurturing the young is divinely a part of creation and rests on principles of ancient provenance far beyond our immediate understanding, then we can have courage in our awesome responsibility as teachers and as parents.

—From remarks made on Parents' Day

November 6, 1976

During the autumn term I have been teaching a course in Shakespeare. As we have read the four great tragedies, I have become more aware than ever that each person's view of the world in which he lives is self-fulfilling in terms of decisions about how to act or how to respond to particular situations.

Macbeth might have waited for chance to crown him. Instead, ambition and wifely pressure lead him to murder Duncan with all the horrible subsequent developments. Othello's jealousy allows Iago to create an apparent infidelity where none existed. Lear's pride and unwillingness to recognize that inevitably one generation follows another carries him to madness. Hamlet's temperamental inclination to intellectualize a matter of revenge results in carnage for the Court of Denmark.

I am not about to suggest that here in chapel this morning sits Macbeth, Othello, Lear, or Hamlet. For that matter, I am not about to suggest that Lady Macbeth, Desdemona, Cordelia, or Ophelia is here either!

What I do have in mind is to explore the ways in which our personal dreams interact, and to look at the ways our ideas about the world around us inevitably interact with other points of view, other people's ideas.

Parents have dreams for their children. Those dreams always look wonderfully larger than life size, and a mother's dreams often differ from a father's.

Many mothers found it easier to accept the changing lifestyles of the late sixties than did fathers because a father sees particularly in his son a reflection of himself, whereas a mother can accept the emergence of someone who seems to be quite different.

Mothers and fathers both, however, tend to think in terms of their own generation. This truth was especially evident in late September when I was meeting with Fifth Form day parents and discussing college application procedures. It became increasingly clear that a number of parents were uneasy; they saw their sons in perspectives more appropriate to an earlier generation. The Acme University father who was accepted for the Class of 1945, when nine out of ten candidates were offered admission, now feels a sense of acute personal rebuff when his son of the Class of 1980 is advised that the acceptance rate is two or three out of ten candidates.

In a more general sense, the Acme University alumnus of 1945 finds it difficult to comprehend that any young person would choose not to go directly on to college from secondary school even though constructive alternatives exist. A year at a British School—three Lawrentians are there now—or a job in a store can be in and of itself a learning experience of significance. It is more than a debatable point as to whether or not all the people now in college really belong there, and furthermore as to whether or not it is essential to go to college to qualify one's self for a rewarding vocation.

Let me suggest just one of many possible bits of evidence on this point. I have no doubt that a significant factor in the college unrest of the late sixties lay in our draft laws, which at that time virtually required a student to remain in college if he did not wish to become subject to the Selective Service process. If young people—if anyone—are locked into a situation neither of their own making, nor of their own choosing, they are likely to break out in unexpected and unprofitable ways.

Teachers are dreamers too. In fact, I cannot think of a better reason for teaching than that one hopes always to create a better person than is ever likely to emerge from the process of education. This means that teachers sometimes expect the impossible and sometimes overlook or fail to provide the proper reward or encouragement to those small victories that inevitably and always are the evidence of ongoing creation. Teachers need to have humility about what they can do and common sense about what they can't. Otherwise, their visions may turn sour, and they can harm students in their care by creating false pressures.

Students, too, have dreams. What wonderful dreams they are: to go to the moon—to make a million dollars—to be President of the United States—to be lovingly married—to square a circle. Wonderful dreams, all of which have in them the essential drive of truth, none of which involves the whole truth of reality.

Quite properly, the dreams and visions of the young are wilder, more grandiose, and less substantial than the dreams of their elders, whether parent or teacher. In fact, it is a large part of the adult's job to help the young to understand reality, where push finally comes to shove.

The young, who are your sons at Lawrenceville, are not just adults who haven't yet reached the legal drinking age. They are the *young,* and that we sometimes forget. They search and test for reality. They are intensely narcissistic, and, therefore, have an imperfectly developed sense of the interrelationships of human affairs. In these critical years, the outer controls of childhood years must be supplanted by an inner gyroscope of high reliability. In the same way, during these critical years, the self-centered fantasy dreams of youth must give way to a shaped and intelligent understanding of the human condition as learned from experience in the Houses, on teams, and in the classroom; as learned in a more direct sense from history and from characters in English as well as from the even more direct function of value teaching within the school community.

The dreams of parents, of teachers, and of students usually overlap, but seldom coincide. Those of you who have some knowledge of celestial navigation will know what I mean by the phrase "the cocked hat." When the navigator has taken his sights, he plots sight lines on his chart. They rarely intersect. In fact, if three sights cross at the same point on the chart, that is almost by definition an indication of an error somewhere! Usually, the three plotted lines cross reasonably close to each other; there is a small triangle, and one presumes that the vessel's position is within that triangle.

As we think about young people growing up, we have to take into account three different lines of sight, three different patterns of dreams, and three different visions that somehow have to be brought together as we evaluate and make judgments about what is happening to a young person in the process of maturing. Though they may from time to time appear to point in quite different directions, all three perspectives have the same purpose.

—From remarks made on Parents' Day

November 12, 1977

Though the pattern has changed somewhat over the years, we have always had as a principal part of Parents' Day a non-denominational service here in Edith Memorial Chapel.

One reason for meeting here is to give parents an impression of what happens in chapel, just as meeting in classrooms provides an opportunity for parents to have some sense of the physical presence of their sons' teachers and of what it is like to sit around one of our conference plan tables.

I am all too conscious, however, that religion is having a difficult time among young people everywhere and in particular at Lawrenceville. Gone are the days of dutiful mass attendance at daily morning chapel, and of Sundays when the gallery would be filled with boys. The chief reason for the change is that America has become a secular Sahara, with precious few oases bubbling with spiritual life; and Lawrenceville is part of American society.

Without exploring why these changes have taken place, let me say simply that I think some good things have happened too. When chapel was filled with boys—in the latter days chiefly as an exercise of discipline—courses in religion generated acute hostilities. Now we are offering more courses, and, in fact, have increased our staff, because of the strong interest shown by boys. But back again to those days of compulsorily filled chapel pews. It was a splendid thing to see, until one began to think about boys who were required to be there, even though their faiths differed from the common denominator, Protestant nature of our services. We now have a Mass said in this chapel on Sunday mornings and Jewish services on campus as well.

This morning I would like to share some thoughts with you about religious training. The ground is treacherous. No subject has generated a thicker fog of factitious generalizations. I take the risk, however, partly because I think it is an important subject and one that not many of us have done much clear thinking about, and partly because it is a subject from which we too frequently retreat with hushed and reverent ignorance all too evident. Finally, it is a parent's proper obligation to think carefully about religious training.

These thoughts came together for me last Saturday morning—just a week ago—when I was attending a meeting of the Canadian Head Masters' Association. I represented American schools in my capacity as President of our Head Masters' Association, but I was also a working member of a series of seminars. One of them focused on the question: "What does it mean to be a Christian school?"

Historically, the answer is simple. A Christian school is one that professes a denominational relationship. "That is a Methodist school," we might say. Or, "They are Quakers." And some of our finest schools rest their programs on a denominational allegiance.

If we go beyond what the catalogue says, we might make further tests of that denominational commitment. Specific rituals of piety and forms of liturgy might be used within a school program to express a conviction. Pushing a little harder, one might then ask, "Ah, yes, I see the name of the denomination, and observe that the forms of piety and worship are being observed, but what lies behind those practices? What actually happens to the human being?"

There we are on even more difficult ground because we would have to identify a shift in sense of self that took place because of a particular program. Is there an ethical goodness that comes through? Or perhaps a particular kind of saintliness?

Very shortly we would find ourselves in the classic situation—to use classic language—of trying to decide whether men are justified by their works or by their faith. If men are justified by their works—the good things they do—they are then given the power of buying their way into heaven, whether or not they have any faith. Conversely, if men can reach heaven solely through acts of faith, they may be lamentably indifferent to those good deeds that ought to characterize a truly religious human being.

I do not propose this morning on this happy day to delve further into scholastic thinking about religious matters. Rather I would like to turn to a completely different way of responding to the question, "What kind of spiritual life is there at Lawrenceville?" Here, I think, we can be on much more specific ground. I also think that in this area school and parent have absolute identity of purpose. We are not really talking about what goes on here in Edith Memorial Chapel, though that too may have its significance; rather we are talking about our understanding of the young person growing up, and our understanding also of adult responsibility for training young people. So my answer has to do with the structure of the school, rather than with the events that take place in Edith Memorial Chapel. At the same time, I think of the matrix that parents provide within the home. Both school and parents are always less than they should be, and capable of a grievous—even harmful—error. Neither school nor parent knows always and in every situation just what is the right thing to do or how to do it. Some principles are clear, however, and I think it is important to set them forth.

The first principle is that God creates. We do not. We can have only a share in the act of creation, and we must ever avoid the temptation of trying to be God-like in relationship with our children. If we try to make them what they cannot be, what they will not be, or what they are not equipped to be, we are likely to damage them, and even more likely to create difficult problems for ourselves. God creates. We are only partners.

Secondly, the young themselves are divine. One of our contemporary absurdities is to become confused about the distinctions between adults and children. Most adults really are adults: more experienced, more completely educated, better balanced, and more emotionally stable than children. One never ought to send a child to do a parent's work, even though we see that happening at least symbolically in contemporary society frequently. On the other hand, the self-satisfied, tin-ear adult who knows all the answers and has the eternal verities chiseled in his forehead, is in fact trespassing upon the divinity of the young. A child, a young person, a son at Lawrenceville, is as magnificently divine as a violet standing in a spring field. The thought comes from Hamlet, "A violet in the primy youth of nature."

Thirdly, we must accept the certainty of failure and of hurt. A school or a parent can readily arrange things so that there is little risk of upset or damage. We can organize every last minute of time, and set up barriers that can only be crossed with extraordinary effort and under extraordinary pressures. We can put distances between generations by talking rather than listening. When we try to protect ourselves from the hurts of being an adult, we are depriving the young of a healing salve of acceptance.

Fourthly, use affirmation rather than prohibition as a means of growth. Education of the young must be an open door toward growth rather than a set of closed doors that stunt it. One characteristic of our age is that, even in the largest matters, fear and knowledge are coupled hand in hand. The knowledge of atomic physics cannot be separated from the thought of atomic warfare. The prospect of genetic engineering cannot be accepted without recognizing risks of infinite enormity. In a smaller scale, the young men who are your sons have before them an extraordinary spectrum of choices. The spectrum of dangers is equally great, but we cannot save them from those dangers by keeping doors closed and confining them to windowless rooms.

Lastly, human beings need each other as flowers need sunlight. There is a cliché phrase that one hears on this campus. A particular boy seems somehow not to be performing up to expectations, and two faculty members talk about him in a department room. They conclude, "He needs some sunshine." What they mean is that he needs attention. He needs to be cared for. He needs to be reached out to. That's what the faculty's job is in every context: classroom, athletic field, theater, activity, and especially the House.

These principles are the ideals of Lawrenceville. I don't know whether you could draw the conclusion from them that Lawrenceville is a Christian school, but I think that question in a way is irrelevant. We try to be sure that what happens is basically sound and right as we provide a matrix for the growth of young people to adulthood.

A school is one facet of God's creation. The relationship between parents and children is another. The two have much in common. I am grateful that you have sent us your sons and am pleased that you have come here today to have some sense of what is happening.

We share today a conscious sense of our responsible participation in the divine act of creation. I find that a thrilling experience, as do my colleagues, and I am sure that every parent here today has had similar feelings. To be part of creation is to achieve a kind of immortality.

—From remarks made on Parents' Day

No one can doubt that our schools are in a mess today. Young people are not learning basic skills of reading and writing. Their College Board scores sag downwards on a toboggan slide; they dress like bums; their speech and manners lack polish.

Given these circumstances, the job that teachers have before them is clear-cut. We must teach reading, writing, and mathematical skills with absolute firmness. We must jack up performance on the College Board verbal scores. We must insist upon greater diligence and clear-cut goal orientation. We must tackle sloppiness in speech and dress. If we can achieve these ends, we shall have ensured a better future for our country and for the world.

Who in this room would argue with the conclusion that our schools are in a mess? Who in this room can quarrel with my diagnosis, or with the remedies that I have suggested? Well, if you want to know who in this room would argue with those conclusions, I am here to tell you that I would be the first! The older I grow, the more concerned I become that both the analysis and the conclusions may be entirely wrong. They may indeed be devastatingly in error. Two specific events of recent months have led me to choose this topic and to develop it from some remarks that I made last autumn to our Lawrenceville parents.

The first event has to do with my reading some comments about a young person growing up. When he was very young, there was concern as to whether or not he was of adequate intelligence because he did not begin talking until the age of three. Later on, in high school, he rebelled at the inflexible system of rote learning, and the demanding manner of his teachers.

One of them said, "You will never amount to anything." Eventually he dropped out of school and spent a year hiking in the mountains, visiting relatives, and touring museums. Finally, however, he pulled himself together and sought admission to a famous institute of technology but failed the entrance exam. After a year of special study, he was admitted, only to cut lectures, read what he pleased, tinker in laboratories, and incur again the wrath of his teachers, one of whom at this level called him "a lazy dog." The only reason he passed his exams and graduated was that a good friend shared careful notes with him.

Having antagonized all of his professors, he failed to obtain a university job and eked out a living by doing odd jobs of tutoring, and of substituting as a teacher until he finally managed a bureaucratic appointment quite unrelated to the education he was supposed to have had.

Some of you will have recognized the person whose educational life I have described. Let's review it quickly: late talker, failed out of high school, took a year off, cut lectures and got his teachers mad at the university level, couldn't get a job. The quotes that I used are all verbatim about the man in question. I am speaking of Albert Einstein as described in the February 19th issue of *Time Magazine*. Education didn't seem to do very much for him!

Let's turn to a second example. This one on a larger scale, and this time there won't be any trickery. I found the fall of the Shah of Iran an incredible event. A seventy-eight-year-old man who had not been in the country for fourteen years went up against the Shah, who was possessed of tanks, guns, and planes unnumbered, who had a powerful secret police at work, and who had a virtual corner on the wealth of his country.

The fact that the tables turned so dramatically, and so totally, provided for me—among other things—new evidence of the age-old truth that man does not live by bread alone, that guns, and tanks, and planes may not be the most powerful weapons in the world. To put a slightly different spin on it, perhaps a religion may have transcending power over human beings.

The visible values of our society suggest the opposite. The Shah should never, by any stretch of the imagination, have been deposed. He had all the cards in his hands, at least all the obvious cards. Einstein should never have become the genius that he was. Everything that schools and colleges tried to do, he resisted, and, in fact, defeated. Where does that leave us? I think that leaves us looking for an invisible set of values, values that we have tended in this pragmatic country and in this technological society to ignore.

Is it possible to see academic achievement, high College Board scores, and polished speech and dress, as being cultural measures inherently hostile to the best qualities of human nature? Be careful to listen to what I am saying. All of the attributes that I have specified are helpful in making a living if you mean that making a lot of money is the same thing as making a living. All of the attributes are comfortable if you mean by comfortable an ease with an essentially dehumanizing industrial society. All of the attributes are helpful if you believe that getting ahead of someone else is inherently good. All of the attributes are helpful if you think that the name of the game is to make money. Quite clearly the conventional criteria, the visible values that schools express, lead to a solid, materialistic life. Is that all there is? That is the question I would like to ask this afternoon.

Let me turn back now to the narrower concern of the teacher. In our schools we implicitly provide moral instruction of one sort or another, though we are much less willing to make the nineteenth century assumption that any school should inherently be concerned with character building. Nevertheless, no school can count for much if it does not include deep concern for growth in terms of character.

That's easier said than done. The gross materialism of our times is devastatingly attractive and has accomplished undeniably much that is good. Under the circumstances, however, how can anyone believe, for example, that giving is better than getting?

The scientific-technical part of our culture proclaims as virtue precisely that detachment from responsibilities that has historically been considered the worst of vices. We see an atomic detonation as an explicit triumph of man's intellect. We disregard what the human consequences may be. We pacify villages with machine guns.

Recent history and current political doctrines accepted by a large proportion of the earth's population suggest that there is no moral value external to the state or to individual experience. "Tell me," said Bonaparte, "how many divisions does the Pope have?" How then can we approach the crucial business of teaching values?

One simple answer is to say that we teach values by living them. An axiom for adults is that we teach by what we are. Indeed it is true that young people have more need of models than of critics. They have more need of sensible adults in their environment than of any number of guide books to moral choice. "Do as I do" is infinitely more important than "Do as I say."

We need not, however, shrink from trying to teach values by speaking of them. If traditional liturgical forms and symbols have diminished in significance, that makes attitudes, understandings, and perspectives derived from study and discussion all the more important. Too frequently, we confine our concern for principles to large, handsome Sunday buildings, which are conspicuously not being used for six days of the week. All human endeavor has moral components for those who are convinced that life is more than a barnyard complex of behavioral responses.

We teach values also by offering trust. Let me explain what I mean by that. If all morality could be encompassed within a rule book like Mao's *Little Red Book,* or like the Ten Commandments, it would be a simple matter to teach young people about values and principles. Human history suggests, however, that righteous adherence to codified laws tends towards destruction of individuals and quickly becomes tyrannically immoral. The New Testament showed a thornier path that does not offer easy rules or sure rewards. Rather it suggests that each person is divine: each parent, each student, each teacher.

The divinity comes from God's love extended to all human beings. When we try to codify that love, we are merely using our own egocentric vision to trap our Maker into a convenient straightjacket. Too much about parenting and teaching is merely a matter of convenience to parent and teacher.

Let's be quite specific about this matter, even though character may not be a particularly fashionable word today. Richard Wear in a recent essay remarked:

Several millennia ago, Heraclitus of Ephesus observed that character is destiny, and nothing has occurred since to render this claim obsolete. Character, that unique feature of humankind that comprises principles, standards, and values is shaped by a limited number of individuals, among whom we may count educators.

I would add parents. We parents and teachers too frequently define the young who are in our care in terms of academic success or failure; high College Board scores or low ratings; class rank (a purely relative measure); Ivy League college admission or some unmentionable alternative; neckties, on or neckties, off; and polished speech or rough.

It is quite possible to score high in all of the categories I have mentioned: academic success, high Board scores, top class rank, Ivy League admission, neckties properly applied, and polished speech. It is quite possible to score high on all these categories and at the same time to have a poorly developed or crippled character. If we define ourselves in the absence of value judgments, we may well find ourselves defining nothing but superficial characteristics.

If we do not pay attention to the invisible values, to character building, we shall have only ourselves to blame for the future that our children will inherit. Have we moved too far from truth, beauty, virtue, love, compassion, tenderness, and faith? Have we instead substituted some much more visible, pragmatic values of what works: what's in it for me?; power is right; if I don't see it, I don't believe it. We are losing the civil part of our civilization, and I think we can see it all around us.

Make no mistake about it. I do not myself take that challenge lightly, and am myself as much in the grip of twenty-first century materialism as anyone in this room, but it gives me pause. I think of Einstein, the student who really didn't make it in schools. I think of the Shah who had all the power of a materialistic world at his finger tips. The lessons of the time are unavoidable.

—From remarks to the Nassau Club

November 1, 1980

I have positive feelings about the School this year and hope that you will also have a sense of those positive feelings as you spend the day with us. When I speak of a positive spirit, what I have in mind is that the young men who are your sons have shown evidence of making right choices not because rules and admonitions constrict their choices, but because they have good inner gyroscopes and want to make the right decisions as they navigate the treacherous channels and dangerous crosscurrents of the adolescent years.

More and more, I am convinced that the principal objective of all education is to liberate the young person, to set him free—even from his own parents—so that he can lead a responsible and intelligent life after his graduation from Lawrenceville. Only three months after receiving his diploma here, a young man goes to college, where he will have very little guidance and a great many conflicting pressures. He had better by that time be able to make decisions for himself on the basis of his own experience and inner convictions.

More years ago than I now care to remember, I took our daughter, Ann, our oldest child, by the hand to walk her to her first year in school, which happens to be across the street and two blocks away from Foundation House. As we neared the school building, I could feel that her hand was restless in mine, and I was sufficiently sensitive to recognize that what she wished to do was to go ahead on her own and to meet whatever might lie ahead in kindergarten. I dropped her hand.

In this school community, your son leads a life of his own without daily parental control. He is learning to be free. Only in that way can he learn to stand on his own two feet. That is one of the invaluable learning experiences unique to a residential community.

There are other ways in which the objective of a Lawrenceville education is to set your son free. Clearly he must, first of all, be free from ignorance. The basic skills of reading, writing, and arithmetic are essential if one is to move easily and effectively within our complicated technological world. It is both the school's and the student's first responsibility to become competent in basic disciplines.

Another attribute of a residential community is that it offers opportunities to try out all kinds of new situations and new roles so that a student can find areas of competence and of self-confidence, with the end result of feeling comfortable about himself so that he can move into new areas and new social situations as opportunity may offer.

To be given a world of one's own as a student does not mean that either parent or faculty member must withdraw entirely. The embryonic world of independent decision making is governed more than most of us realize by the presence of adult experience and attitudes. The steadying adult influence can be expressed in many ways: high expectations are much more significant than impassioned exhortations; clear examples are much more important than intellectual exposition; faith in the young is a much more effective means of creating confidence than suspicion about failure; and nervous precautions and

84

prescriptions given to our sons convey to them the message that we lack confidence in them and are not prepared to consider them responsible.

We must also recognize that when the young are on their own, there inevitably are mistakes. Thomas Aquinas observed "The good angels do not entirely restrict the bad angels from inflicting harm." Perhaps it is my age that is showing, but I am inclined to think that the number of the bad angels has increased during my years as a teacher. Having said that, however, I think it is true that the good angels have also increased. Contemporary society presents our young people with many more opportunities than were available to their parents. Those are the good angels. It also presents to young people many more dangers. Those are the bad angels.

The image that comes to mind is the picture of trying to make landfall on shore on a dark night where there are many lights. Though there may be visible ahead only two beacons that can be of significant help as we try to make the harbor, there are myriad other lights that confuse us, and that may lead us into trouble. Particularly for the inexperienced, the problem of making a safe landfall is extraordinarily difficult. And that, I think, is where the close relationship of a boy to his housemaster, to a section master, or to some other member of the faculty who can be helpful in counseling is especially important.

Ironically that is also where a parent often cannot be tremendously helpful because a boy emerging into manhood inevitably must distance himself from his parents. So there we are back again with the subject of setting a young man free, particularly from his parents.

That may be, and indeed is, precisely what a parent wants. He wishes his child to become a man, to be able to move independently, confidently, and creatively into the world of adult life. Yet the precise point of letting go is terribly difficult to determine, and there can be no easy guidebook to tell anyone just how to do that.

For the parents, it is important to have faith in their children. If parents express doubt rather than confidence, they will deprive their children of the freedom that leads to a strong sense of responsibility. If children cannot give some earnest of their own sense of responsibility through genuine accomplishment, no matter how insignificant, then the faith will be surely tried. But if I had to choose between faith and works in the matter of young people growing up, I would unhesitatingly bet on faith because I believe absolutely that sooner or later the silver cord must be broken; sooner or later the child must make his own decisions; sooner or later the young person must begin to assume responsibility; and sooner or later the young person must be put on his own.

I am absolutely convinced that a young person must have the faith of his parents and of his school if he is to grow to that kind of freedom that alone can make a responsible adult.

—From remarks made on Parents' Day

October 31, 1981

On a blue-bright, early morning in mid-July of last summer, I sailed south on the Hudson River from the 79th Street Marina. My companion and I were headed around Manhattan, up the East River, and out the Long Island Sound through Hell Gate. Because tides at Hell Gate are dangerous, timing was important. We arrived at the Battery about a half-hour early just to make sure that we would be making the passage up the East River at exactly the correct moment.

With half an hour to spare, we sailed south to the Statue of Liberty. She is a grand lady. There she stood on her island towering over us. Though there was a light mist on the water, the sky above was deep blue. Golden-warm sunlight of the early hours played on her torch. As we sailed out to Bedloe's Island, my companion and I were deeply moved.

We were moved, not by the size of the statue, nor even by the circumstances of the gift of French school children, but by the idea of what she stands for. The Statue of Liberty stands for the freedom that we Americans so richly enjoy, and so much take for granted.

Many years ago, Marshall McLuhan observed that it probably wasn't a fish that discovered water. How could he? He took it for granted, and it was all around him. Similarly, Americans take freedom for granted. It is all around us. We have nothing to compare it with. This morning I would like to consider four ideas about freedom as they relate to parents, to sons, and to schools.

First of all, the freedom that we enjoy as Americans was largely a gift earned for us by others. This great school is a gift from preceding generations, and we in turn have the responsibility for it. It is not ours to possess. It is ours to nurture.

So parenthood is a gift from parents who have gone before us and of a Creator. Our sons are divine in the sense that we are part of them and they of us, but their potential goes beyond what we can imagine. We must not try selfishly to make them into brittle images of ourselves. Rather we must allow the divine spark within them to do its protean work even though that certainly means surprise and separation from us.

It follows that a school stands somewhere between the parent and the child, encouraging the divine spark without actually knowing what will develop. We have no prescription for your children. We have no blueprint. What we do have is faith in their ultimate growth to maturity and the understanding that they cannot grow unless we get out of their way and, at the same time, provide the challenges, resources, and opportunities that create a matrix for development.

Secondly, the freedom that we enjoy accepts the tensions of diversity: of cultures, ideals, and religious convictions. The weak, the insecure, and the small-minded always turn away from diversity because it is hard to live with. Petty tyrants in business, politics, or the church seek simple, black-and-white patterns that deny diversity and destroy the dynamism of tension.

So parenthood must accept tensions. The young grow up by definition in a world different from their parents'. We remember the good things of our adolescent years and forget the difficulties. We like to think that we ought to be able to abolish the tensions of diversity by declaring either that they're not there or that we don't accept them, but life is a process of breaking away, one generation from another. It is always painful and always hard to understand.

What that means for a school is that we can never be as neat and tidy as we would like, that we must always keep in mind the circumstance that we are teaching people, not books, even though we use books to teach people. Furthermore, we cannot adopt the beguiling robes of prophets because we, as teachers, then succumb to the temptation of believing that our own egos are so powerful that we need not pay attention to anyone else. There are too many ten-hour teachers.

Thirdly, there is something bigger than factories, freeways, fudge, F16s, and the Federal Reserve System. The human spirit is bigger. A totally materialist world has no need for freedom because it is convinced that each human being is simply a cog in a world of things. The Poles are working out that problem this very day.

There is no need for freedom in a static, arbitrary, dictatorial society, whether the tyranny is religious, economic, or political. So it is that the aim of a Lawrenceville education is to set your sons free because they are divine. We cannot make them in our image. The traditional way in the western world of expressing this truth is to say that every man is in the image of God, *imago dei;* what that means is that a school must set young people on right courses and get out of their way.

Fourthly, the freedom that we enjoy has survived because Americans have been willing to work for it. Indifference and smugness are the sins that have the power of destroying us. Passionate caring and willingness to make a commitment are the lifeblood elements of continuing freedom.

So, parenthood is something much more than a rational business proposition or an inevitable physiological event. In one act, it expresses all of the relationships between two people along with all of their ancestors together with all of their descendants. The relationship grows not so much because of prudence and sheltering as because of caring and commitment. Blandness can breed only blandness. We must be caring.

So it is that a school sees its responsibility for setting young people free by equipping them with appropriate disciplines in the perspective of the long history of mankind. The school in some sense is an extension of the family. In another sense, it is an extension of society. In fact, that is where family and society meet, and the ultimate purpose of both is somehow to make a difference in the lives of the young people entrusted to them.

Finally, I see all of us, parents, teachers, and students, as being motivated by a fundamental desire to become immortal by somehow making a difference in the lives of others. To that end, we transmit disciplines of a basic sort like reading, writing, and arithmetic. To that end, we try to develop self-confidence so that our children can accept diversity. To that end, we seek to convince the young in our care that there is more to the world than mere things and ensure that they know they must care about the world they live in and take an active part in it.

Parent, school, son: all are involved in this business of freedom. That is why I am thinking this morning of the Statue of Liberty on a lovely July morning.

The Statue of Liberty stands there because generations of Americans have committed themselves to making a difference. We can do no less. We can do no more. That is our great privilege.

—From remarks made on Parents' Day

PART V
Endings

June 4, 1961

---

*"And Jesus said unto him, If thou wilt be perfect, go and
sell that thou hast, and give to the poor, and thou shalt
have treasure in heaven"—Matthew 19:21*

The rich man of this morning's scripture lesson is familiar to anyone
who has the slightest acquaintance with the Christian tradition. Jesus says,
"Go, sell what you have, and give to the poor, and you will have treasure in
heaven." We all would agree that Jesus has asked a momentous sacrifice and
that through such complete rededication a man may truly discover his
relationship with God, but how does one make that sacrifice in a highly
specialized, highly compartmentalized, highly industrial and technological
society? It was a simpler day when a man could give up his fortune to follow
Jesus. People are substantially the same, but circumstances have certainly
changed.

There is much talk these days of sacrifice, of giving, and of decaying
morality. All the world's ills—from the debacle in Cuba to the rising tide of
inflation and taxes—are blamed on someone who didn't sacrifice something or
on someone who regarded it as more blessed to receive than to give. Precisely
who has failed and in what manner he has been less than he should be is
seldom specified. Few of us, of course, would regard ourselves as being
deliberately selfish or as deliberately shirking our responsibilities. The fact
remains, however, that the world seems to be in kaleidoscopic chaos.
Obviously, there is something wrong somewhere and most of us are very
uneasy about our responsibility for the mess, though we are at a loss to
discover just how we have failed. We are at a loss and uneasy because this
matter of giving has many turnings.

For one thing, the mere act of sacrifice to a larger purpose has no inherent
virtue and may lead to evil as well as to good. Mr. Eichmann is on trial in
Israel for murdering with precision and dispatch some millions of European
Jews. Whatever the decision of the court in Jerusalem may be, it is just
common sense that a great many other supposedly intelligent and civilized
people were accomplices in a program of barbarity that dwarfs prior instances
of bestiality as an atomic explosion dwarfs the first Chinese firecracker.
Eichmann's own defense is his devotion to higher authority, and I am sure that
in his own mind this argument provides sufficient justification. So also did his
subordinates give themselves to their grisly tasks with the thought that they
were serving some higher purpose. Devotion to the Fatherland was a powerful
force, which in this case brought about a holocaust.

I have heard it said of this general thesis that it may well have been true
in Hitler's Germany, but "it could never happen here." To the contrary, I
believe with all my heart and mind—repugnant as the thought may be—that
it *could* happen here. To think otherwise is to hide one's head in the sand.

Given a sufficiently malevolent leader with a magnetic personality, our nice, gentle, suburban Americans could be brought to participate in barbarities beyond our most macabre imagination. The career of Huey Long provides a specific example of what *can, could,* and *may* happen here.

The capacity for evil has always existed by the side of the power for good. In fact, the question, "What is good?" is only the reverse side of the question, "What is evil?" It's a very much like the old scholastic conundrum, "Is heat the absence of cold, or is cold the absence of heat?" This is a more difficult question than it at first seems to be, and it inevitably raises the further question of whether or not cold and heat are two different things, or are they one and the same? We are not ourselves scholastics, and I shall not develop the parallel to explore the separate identities of good and evil. What I do wish to emphasize—whatever else may be true—is that good and evil always exist together.

There is nothing new in this generalization about good and evil. One finds it implicit in the Old and New Testament and in most of the world's religions. There *is* something new, however, in the dimensions involved. The incredible growth in man's mastery of his environment has pushed the possibilities of good and of evil to an ultimate dimension. It can now be said with cool, rational certainty that one foolish man could annihilate the entire human race—or one determined man, or one careless man, or one ignorant man—but most particularly, one evil man could end the human experiment once and for all. Finally.

We are greater men in a very real sense. We have a greater God and a greater Satan. We come close to the situation in a truism we often use in another context. "The bigger they are, the harder they fall," we sometimes say. My thought is that we could well substitute the first person pronoun "we" for the third person "they." "The bigger we are, the harder we fall."

Part of the difficulty in seeing this predicament is that the extraordinary mastery we have over our environment misleads us into thinking that we exercise a corresponding control over ourselves. There was a time when there was a meaningful relationship between cold weather and the aching muscles of a bicep flexed long hours in splitting firewood. There was a time when there was a direct link between the distance a man had traveled and the soles of his feet. There was a time when beefsteak on the table meant cleaning out the guts of a carcass hanging from a tree. The thermostat, the automobile, and the meat packers have profoundly modified these relationships. To take but one more example, consider carefully the extraordinary phenomenon of a fat-belly prosperity that allows us to make a fetish of a food, or consider the product "Metrecal", which prevents us from eating too much of what we have too much of. Similarly extraordinary phenomena echo and re-echo through our society, and we must recognize them for what they are.

Our industrial society has another consequence that is just as dangerous as the ultimates of power and as the divorce from environment that I have mentioned. We run a great risk of totally isolating ourselves from one another. Look at an orderly pile of round, shiny containers in a warehouse. What do they contain? Aerosol? Fancy sliced peaches? Chef Boy-ar-dee's spaghetti dinner? Whatever it may be it is uniform, rationalized, standardized, and reduced to the common denominator of the machine age. Now look at another regimented pile of square, shiny, containers. Boxes for cookies perhaps? Or could they be boxes for people? Like, for example, the new skyscrapers on Upper Park Avenue? The parallel is sufficiently close so that I am appalled by what I see in this area as well as elsewhere. The functionalist architect says that his forms are logical. They are indeed, and the logic of his buildings is a symbol of what I fear. Scientific accomplishment must serve man, not vacuum pack him in a lonely uniformity.

We speak often of the marvels of modern communication, and it is unquestionably exciting to dial San Francisco from New Jersey or to watch the launching of Commander Shepherd from his pad at Cape Canaveral. But here too it seems to me that there are concomitants that ought to be faced fairly and fully. What good does it do to know all about the plight of a burning ship in the Persian Gulf when we know little and care less about what is happening outside our front door? Our curiosity about people remote from us is so avid that we have created a press, a radio system, and TV networks that creep into every crevice of personal and public life without regard for privacy or policy. This is the reverse of freedom; it is license, and it generates more heat than light.

I have just finished reading Dickens' *Bleak House* with my Fifth Form section, and one phrase in it keeps ringing in my mind. You may remember Mrs. Jellyby, who had flocks of children and a very untidy house. She was an extraordinarily energetic woman who ignored her immediate responsibilities because she was more interested in the natives of BoorioBoola-GHA, ironically located in the Congo. No matter that she lacked the slightest knowledge of Africa. No matter that any fraud could take advantage of her benevolence. She sacrificed her family and ignored many real and immediate evils to remedy a supposed evil that was far away. She gave herself totally to her concern for African natives. Dickens calls this "telescopic philanthropy."

The adjective "telescopic" serves as a transition to my conclusion. Our powers are such that we tend to think big, to look distances, and to give ourselves to broad, find generalizations. We properly hitch our wagons to stars, but are we always sure about the next step? Would Mr. Eichmann, the person—the unique individual under God—be in a prisoner's dock in Jerusalem today had he looked more nearly at what he was doing? Or to put it another way, is it possible that we under similar circumstances might have reacted similarly? Emotionally I reject the possibility at once. Rationally I must admit to doubts. The ultimates of power reduce us to insignificance as individuals. The nature of our environment divorces us from reality of the most primitive and essential sort. Standardization threatens to isolate us in monotonous sameness and make us incapable of essential integrity as individuals. Our means of information put us on misleading trails.

Much of what I have said has an admonitory quality and well it should. I am prepared to stand fully and firmly by what I have said about the characteristics of our highly sophisticated industrial society. It seems to me to be something new in the world and something that we must learn to master. Happily, the means of coming to terms with it are at hand, though with sacrifice of a sort very different from that which Mr. Eichmann invokes as his motive. The sacrifice required is above all immediate and personal. We know that the grass on the other side of the fence is always greener in terms of opportunity. It is correspondingly true that the grass is greener on the other side in terms of sacrifice and responsibility. We love to fight other people's battles and tend to ignore our own because they are less obvious, less dramatic, and very much more difficult. Our best hope lies in our individual devotion to the tasks and relationships that are immediately ours. More distant obligations have their place, but the first and more important rededication is to the immediate and the personal.

Gentlemen of the graduating Class: As Lawrentians shortly to receive your diplomas, you have paid attention to the business at hand. In varying degrees you have accepted the personal challenge of long, slow, patient, hard, difficult, nagging, frustrating work and have come up for more. To a greater or lesser extent you have dedicated yourselves and the qualities uniquely yours to the responsibilities uniquely yours. The assignment, the class recitation, a high B flat on a trumpet, or service as a council member, these are the first things.

What then follows is a sense of principle in all of the immediate things that we do. You know what the principles are. I need only briefly touch upon them: the fatherhood of God, the brotherhood of man, and the unique divinity of the individual. When these are imminent in our lives—not as through a telescope, distantly—then we shall have shared the human birthright of both good and evil. It is not easy and never has been easy. That is why it requires sacrifice, and this is where we must all begin. Having begun well, we can then say in the face of a challenging and sometimes menacing world that, "With men it is impossible, but not with God; for all things are possible with God."

—From the Baccalaureate Address

June 2, 1968

At the opening convocation in December, I spoke of self-discovery as the great end of all learning. I used then the familiar passage from Paul's First Letter to the Corinthians: "At present we are men looking at puzzling reflections in a mirror. The time will come when we shall see reality whole and face to face."

Today I return both to the theme of self-discovery and to Paul. The narrative of Saul's conversion to Christianity is a particularly dramatic example of a process—traditionally called education—that involves a series of self-discoveries. Few of us will have experiences of the magnitude or intensity that Saul experienced on the road to Damascus. If we are growing at all, however, we are likely to say, as one Fifth Former did last week, "My point of view has changed. I see things in a different perspective as a consequence of my Lawrenceville education."

"I see things in a different perspective." How many members of the Fifth Form can say that this morning? How many have learned enough about themselves this year so that their point of view has changed? I would not seek a cataclysmic conversion like Paul's; rather I would hope for these small changes in points of view that reflect increasing maturity in understanding of self.

Let's look again for a moment at Saul's conversion. What really had changed? Was he physically different afterwards? Did the road sign still say "Damascus"? Was the sky bluer? Had old friends disappeared? The fact is, of course, that nothing had changed; nothing had changed except Saul. His perception of the world around him had shifted radically. He had a new perspective.

The truth is that our understanding of the world around us is an intensely self-centered affair. Let me illustrate with two familiar aphorisms. We say, for example, "He sees everything through rose-colored spectacles." Or we remark solemnly, "An optimist says a water glass is half full; a pessimist says it's half empty."

How are *your* spectacles tinted this morning? How would *you* describe that water glass? Answer those questions, and I'll be on the way to knowing some basic things about you *and* about your education. Tell me, how do you look at this chapel, at your roommate, at your math teacher, at Peter Forte's sideburns? When you give me the answers, I'll know something about you but not necessarily much about chapel, your roommate, your teacher, or sideburns.

Many of our perceptions, of course, are prescribed by external authority. Parents are first and foremost in helping us to organize our first years of experience; but as we become increasingly independent, we begin to make the painful transition to our own point of view. Unknowingly, however, we often escape what we take to be our parents' stony inflexibility only to adore dogmatically other forms of external authority. For example, the National Association of Manufacturers, S.D.S., and Karl Marx offer ready-made specifications to mold our perceptions, and the weak in spirit will be content with the pablum of unquestioned orthodoxy.

As you all know even better than I, youthful acceptance of conventional orthodoxy is rather out of fashion today; witness the chaos of Columbia. Instead, every young man must have his "own thing." This intense individualism is perhaps a reaction precisely to the forms of external authority that have been so important to the young of other generations. Reaction though it may be, this individualism, bordering on nihilism, is itself dangerous. Mark Twain made the central point about the still, small voice within. You remember the passage in *Huck Finn* when Huck and Jim are floating down the river. Huck saves Jim's life by telling a lie, and it worries Huck both because he has told a lie and because he knows perfectly well that white boys aren't supposed to think of black boys as human beings.

Huck's conscience bothers him, though from his point of view he has done the right thing in human terms. Finally, he dissolves the dilemma in favor of the right human act and says "If my conscience were a yaller dog I'd kick it." The passage expresses the age old fact that man's conscience is terribly vulnerable. It suggests that whatever your particular "thing" may be—beads or beards or boots—it has little to do with an inner truth.

If the conscience itself is vulnerable to external bias, how much more vulnerable are our everyday perceptions to emotional distortions. A man in a rage is no fit judge of his antagonist. Love can persuade us that one member of the opposite sex is like no other. Sex can convince us that we've discovered love. Fatigue can turn us grumpily against our closest friends. Joy can dissolve personal antagonisms. Desire to share a House football victory can erase sidelines and spectators from our awareness. Guilt can color our reaction to a Discipline Committee decision or a newspaper story of a race riot.

So where do we go from there? How can we learn enough about ourselves to have some reasonable assurance that we're on the right track; to have some confidence in our perception of the world around us?

One way we learn is through those moments of truth that inevitably arise during the course of our year together in this intensely centripetal School community. More often than not, such moments are neither pretty nor pleasant. More often than not, it is the experience of failure that can humanize us in ways that easy successes cannot.

Fifth Formers recognized this fact in terms of college admissions. Several of them have spoken from this platform about the impact of college rejection. I shall not embroider upon what has already been said so well. Let me try to shock you just a bit, however, by saying that those candidates who sailed right through the competition and crossed the line with Harvard, Yale, and Princeton pennants flying high may in the end be the losers.

The "golden boy" syndrome bred of effortless triumphs can destroy self-knowledge just as surely—and perhaps more surely—than repeated failure. Have you ever noticed that people who must live with a severe physical difficulty are often sweeter tempered, more sensitive, and more relaxed than others? To suffer is to learn.

Try another example. Out of the blue, an ice-hardened snow ball smashes into the chest of a boy standing with some classmates waiting to take an exam.

The boy who throws the snowball walks away smirking. "Damned Jew," he says. What did you do? Maybe you chuckled inanely with the bully, who is one of the wheeler dealers on campus.

Maybe you stood by, crushed by the grossness of it all but unable to think that you should become involved. And the victim? Well, *Virtus semper viridis* (for the benefit of those who majored in Greek, virtue is always green, always growing); that's the school motto. How, after all, do you grow virtue except through moments of truth, some of which in retrospect seem pretty shameful?

Other moments of truth come before us in the classroom as we vicariously discover the Hamlet that is in us all, as we argue in a history class about the inevitability of war, or as we enter the new and sometimes terrifying world of ideas. Why is it that of all the animals only men and rats organize to kill their own species—not lions or tigers or mosquitoes or worms—men and rats.

Take *Playboy* magazine. There's a reference I can assume everyone will recognize. Have you ever thought about it this way?

Playboy *really feeds on the existence of a repressed fear of involvement with women. The male identity crisis to which the magazine speaks has at its roots a deep-set fear of sex, a fear that is uncomfortably combined with fascination. Sexuality is reduced to a consumption item, totally accessible but entirely separated from authentic human maturity.*

The passage is from a text sometimes used in Lawrenceville. Has it provided a confrontation for you?

Some moments of truth involve direct crises, some are vicarious. Role playing is yet another way to seek definition of self. A young man unsure of himself will try to become different persons whom he imagines he might like to be. The more unsure he is, the more flamboyant his role playing is likely to be, and we certainly have seen a spate of it on campus this year. Recognizing the central importance of role-playing in self-discovery, an outspoken teacher recently commented, "a school that restricts freedom, invades privacy, and limits enterprise in order to promote normality is certainly not promoting growth."

No one, after all, can tell you, force you, or seduce you for long into seeing the world a certain way. Your perceptions of the world around you rest upon your own understanding of yourself, and that understanding of self comes upon you as miraculously as the vision that came upon Saul as he traveled the road to Damascus.

Selfhood begins with family and society, becomes modified by ideas and emotions, but ultimately grows to maturity in the context of experience and trial and error. Once selfhood begins to take shape, we can have confidence in our understanding of the world around us. Then and then only can we count ourselves educated men.

Gentlemen of the Graduating Class: I hope that each of you can say, "My point of view has changed. I see things in a different perspective as a consequence of my Lawrenceville education." Sensitive and informed perception based on unflinching knowledge of self is the hallmark of a humanely educated man.

You have all seen Frederic Remington's paintings of cowboys and Indians on the western plains. One of the paintings shows two terrified Indians looking up at a towering thunderhead. The title is "The Eye of the Mind," and the point is that Indian fear and superstition have created terrifying portents out of something that we would regard as a routine and perhaps even beautiful natural phenomenon.

What you make of the world will be a consequence of what you perceive the world to be. I cannot tell what tasks you may face in your adult lives. I will be confident, however, of you and of the future if only I can be sure that your perceptions will become sharper and more sensitive in years to come. The process will continue through college and your adult years. I pray that you will understand and accept always those moments of truth that strengthen selfhood and in turn give greater insight to the eye of the mind.

—From the Baccalaureate Address

June 4, 1976

To build a solid, long lasting stone wall, or even a plasterboard partition, you need a plumb line: just a length of cord with a weight tied to the bottom. Never, ever, wrong, this simple device exacerbates because it infallibly shows what's vertical and what's tilted. To an impatient carpenter like me, the plumb line humiliates because it always shows up my mistakes.

The Old Testament prophet, Amos, used the image of a plumb line in one of his visions of judgment:

The Lord stood upon a wall made out of plumb line with the plumb line in his hand, and the Lord said unto me, Amos, what seeest thou? And I said a plumb line. Then said the Lord, and behold, I will set a plumb line in the midst of my people Israel.

Amos talks sense. If we wish to build a house, navigate an ocean, or walk on the moon, we must make all of our decisions with reference to some sort of plumb line. The laws of gravity ensure that our house will stand for generations. The laws of astronomy and of magnetism help us cross an ocean. The laws of celestial mechanics place us on the moon.

We can understand what happens to us and make decisions about where we are headed only in the context of the ideas that we have about what's taking place. Events do not explain themselves. We must see them in perspective.

Take, for example, Sir Isaac Newton. For eons, apples had been falling from trees, and humans had been watching. I like to imagine the afternoon in a sleepy orchard filled with the buzzing of bees when Newton suddenly placed the happening in the context of an idea that he named gravity. Events do not explain themselves. We understand them only in the context of ideas.

In what context then do we understand this Baccalaureate Service, this Commencement, this conclusion to a year, and this educational experience? What does the graduation of the Class of 1976 mean to students, faculty, and parents?

Commencement speakers often see the occasion as a "setting free." Addresses emphasize the commence part of commencement and speak of the beginning of a "brave new world." That idea has certainly had currency among seniors in every year that I have been associated with Lawrenceville. In fact, it had considerable currency when I myself was a senior in a residential school!

"Won't it be great to get out of here! At long last we are free!" As a Fifth Former recently put it to me, most seniors are just interested in "getting out," but I ask the question, "Aren't they really getting in?"

This spring, a line from *The Fantasticks* caught my ear. "Time is the most stringent teacher," said the actor. "Time is the most stringent teacher." Could it be that final examinations, training rules, and the discipline of The Lawrenceville School are far less fierce and unyielding in their demands than the working out of time itself? "Time will tell," they say, and so indeed time does tell. The mills of the Gods grind slow, but they grind exceeding small. Freedom is an idea only superficially pertinent to us on this Commencement Eve.

What else is education for? To put it bluntly, money gives meaning to education. We speak of investing in our education and of repayment in years to come. Thus, a degree from Ivy College earns $5,000 more annual salary than a B.A. from Corn Corners College. A chilling irony balances the degree of truth in that equation. The truth is self-evident, but the irony not.

As F. S. Schumacher points out in his intriguing book, *Small Is Beautiful*, "We preach the virtues of hard work and restraint while painting utopian pictures of unlimited consumption without either work or restraint." To the extent that we speak of the rewards of hard work, we at the same time conceive of those rewards as relief from the burdens of that work and from the ordinary consequences of human responsibility.

In further irony—again quoting from Schumacher—the western world has come to feel a sense of uneasiness about one of its major, animating ideas. Intoxicated by the triumphs of our industrial societies, we have tended to equate possessions with happiness. What we are discovering, however, is that "The production of too many things results in too many useless people." Possession of things—automobiles, cruising sailboats, and chalets in Switzerland—has turned out to be a vacuous measure of human endeavor.

George Orwell had something to say about that possibility when he forecast in *1984* that industrial countries would have to fight mythical wars in uninhabited parts of the planet simply in order to dispose of the fecal matter of industrial societies. We are only eight years from 1984.

Can we see achievement applauded on this Commencement Day as a crucial turning point in mastery of the world around us? Surely we would all agree that ignorance leads to poverty, superstition, and cruelty. Education, by contrast, leads to an easing of the physical limitations of space and time. It makes us all healthier and gets us to the moon on time.

Surely, however, we are all too much aware of the shortcomings of technological management in human affairs, both individually and collectively. The concept that control of our environment through intellect will create a better world simply will not stand up to common sense examination.

The modern western world is too fragile, too brutal, too nervous, too neurotic, too unequal, and too unhappy to permit any of us to feel that more education will inevitably produce a better world.

Not very many years ago, this country believed that all we needed to do to ameliorate social ills was to pump large sums of money into the educational system to produce better educated and, therefore, more employable, less prejudiced Americans. The results seem to indicate that the effort has, to a large extent, gone for naught. Whatever else education may do, it doesn't seem to give people much control over themselves, even if it may give them some control over their environment.

So I return to Amos and to our question. To build well, we need a plumb line. To understand our world, we must hold up beside it a governing idea. If our ideas are small, weak, superficial, and incoherent, our lives—including graduation from Lawrenceville—will appear insipid, uninteresting, petty, and chaotic. I borrow again from Mr. Schumacher and add his observation that when people ask for education, they really are looking for ideas to make the world and their own lives intelligible to them.

Your education at Lawrenceville has taught you something about yourselves and about the world in which you live. Some of that process has been deliberate on the part of your teachers. More of it has been implicit in your participation in the Lawrenceville experience than in classroom instruction, conversations with Housemasters, or addresses from this platform.

Have you equipped yourself with basic human disciplines? Effective reading, skillful writing, and mastery of numbers provide powerful tools that can lead to great achievement.

Have you learned that to do something well that is difficult or painful may in the end be a great joy? Have you had that experience in a French class, at the keyboard of a piano, during an Outward Bound experience, or in trying to get along with a roommate?

Have you learned enough about your inner self to live a contributing life with other human beings? Can you relate person to person without the meddling intrusion of insecurity, insensitivity, and ego?

Gentlemen of the Graduating Class: These questions ultimately become one. Have you begun to discover a plumb line of your own? You will be free now in many senses because education sets you free. What will you do with that freedom? You are likely to prosper because your parents have given you advantages available to few, even in America. What will you build upon those advantages? What will that prosperity mean for you?

—From the Baccalaureate Address

Gentleman of the Graduating Class, tomorrow after the commencement ceremonies you will rejoice because you will be free. No more exercise credits, room inspections, class bells, daily assignments, Discipline Committees, or irritating check-ins. All those irksome impositions that have so vexed you will be gone. Tomorrow you will be free

Tomorrow you will be free in what sense? From what? For what?

Men have asked these questions about freedom since the beginning of time. The Bible, for example, is a history book about setting people free. Adam and Eve make a free choice, and lose the Garden of Eden only to find pain and suffering. Moses cries out to Pharoah, "Let my people go." The Israelites cross the Red Sea to reach the Promised Land but without their leader.

The New Testament also speaks of freedom. Jesus sets his followers free from the pettifogging restrictions that had so captured the Pharisees. Jesus then, through his sacrifice, frees individuals from the burden of guilt for their shortcomings.

In contemporary life, we use the concept of freedom in a positive sense as we speak of the free world, a free society, or the freedom of mankind.

Freedom is a complex subject. We must be careful to look at it the right way. Do you remember that old story about the child who watched a freight train go by and said to his parents, "Look at the red caboose pushing that train."

As we think about freedom, we must be sure that we are examining what makes it work, the engine, rather than some of the remote consequences of spurious freedoms.

How easy it is, first of all, to say what freedom is not. Our first instincts are to make the easy assumption that if we are free our wishes will be granted and our world perfect. Some of you, set free tomorrow will be thinking as you drive away from this campus that you are now, finally, going to the promised land. College lies beyond, and we think of college as a place where everything that has vexed us here at Lawrenceville will have disappeared. It will be a Disneyland of self-indulgence: late sleep, oceans of beer, plenty of "natural" relationships, infrequent quizzes, and all the rest. You know them. So do I. I can still remember those promises of indulgence that sparkled in my imagination on the day when I graduated from school. No infant dreaming of sugar plums on Christmas Eve ever had brighter thoughts about the rewards of college than I did as I set off for my freshman year.

Beyond college lies another vision—a picture of America the beautiful—the suburb with a modest $250,000 home, a beautiful Dior-gowned wife, and a job at a half-million dollars a year, with a personal Gulf Stream II added as a perquisite. What a lovely dream of paradise!

All of us here this evening know, however, that I have taken sight on easy game. Freedom is more than license to do what one wishes. Gratification of our desires carries within it a seed of self-destruction. We all know folk tales that rest upon the idea that to have precisely what one wants is to experience gaping hell itself.

For good reason, the Middle Ages identified Seven Deadly Sins, all of which could be called freedoms: Pride, the freedom to express one's ego at the expense of others; covetousness, the freedom to believe that we ought to have what someone else possesses; lust, the freedom to allow glands to become our captains; anger, the freedom to vent our emotional frustrations without regard to anyone else's feelings; gluttony, the freedom to feed our faces like pigs at troughs; envy, the freedom to wish that we were what we are not; and sloth, the freedom to do nothing.

Pride, covetousness, lust, anger, gluttony, envy, and sloth, these were the Seven Deadly Sins of the Middle Ages. In a sense, they might be said to speak of freedoms. In fact, they speak of license, and we all know that.

Genuine freedom carries with it an adamantine link to responsibility. Members of the Class of 1977 will be free tomorrow not because their lives will be less circumscribed by the necessary disciplines of learning and of living together; rather, they will be free because of what they have been given and because of what they will take away from their Lawrenceville experience. However imperfect, however incomplete, the objective of a liberal arts education is to set people free.

The skills of reading, writing, and numbers that you have strengthened and confirmed at Lawrenceville will free you to learn. The history of mankind, some of which you have learned here, will give you new insights that can free you to contribute more richly to your society. Living with varied others in a residential community and empathizing with all conditions of humanity through reading can free you to have a sensitivity for other individuals as well as for yourself.

Resourcefulness derived from learning varied methods of problem solving employed in different disciplines will free you from narrow answers and help you to understand what the proverb means when it says that there is usually more than one way to skin a cat.

Poetry, art, and music can give you metaphors that free you to place life in a creative context so that you can both enjoy it and give enjoyment to others.

The liberal arts set us free. The self-indulgences of the Seven Deadly Sins entrap us. Freedom is not a matter of doing what we want to do, but of being able to do more than we ever thought might be possible.

To do more than one ever thought possible is to have the power to create. That is the greatest freedom of all. It is the way in which we share with each other, with the past, with the future, and with our Creator. It involves, of course, magnificent responsibility. How we use the freedom to create is in a very practical sense the central question of our time.

In the last three weeks, I have been reading with my Fifth Form English section Shakespeare's *The Tempest*. Most of you remember the plot. Prospero rules over an Eden-like island. His magic wand gives him absolute control over tempestuous seas, good and evil spirits, and survivors from a shipwreck that he has reason to cause at the beginning of the play. His power is unchallenged, and he is human enough to use it. He enjoys the freedom that he has to send a mercurial Ariel on errands hither and yon. He delights in magically providing a groaning banquet table with the snap of his fingers. He exults in being able to paralyze the raised arm of a former enemy who is about to strike him with a sword. When all is said and done, however, Prospero is wise enough to recognize that the self-indulgent exercise of absolute power can result only in a static, sterile, and self-destructive world. Unrestrained freedom that takes the form of license can only become static, sterile, and self-destructive.

Recognizing that he has denied the divinity of creation, Prospero, at the end of *The Tempest,* breaks his wand, knowing that in so doing he is taking a major risk and knowing also that in so doing he joins the human race to become a creative part of it.

The gift of a liberal arts education is a gift of power and of freedom. We of the western world have not always exercised that power well, nor have we always understood the responsibilities that go with it. Ironically, our failure is all the more glaring because the western world has provided the single figure in all history who expresses more graphically than any other the truth that self-indulgent power is self-destructive. I speak, of course, of Jesus of Nazareth, who accepted the world by giving up his life, denying the power that often tempts us in the form of self-indulgent license.

Gentlemen of the Graduating Class: Rejoice. Tomorrow you will indeed be free. In the sense that you will be free from some of the petty bureaucracy of Lawrenceville, I share your sense of exhilaration. In the largest perspective, however, I urge you to rejoice not so much because you will be moving to new arenas of possible self-indulgence as to recognize that it is from your education within the liberal arts tradition that your most important freedom will grow.

—From the Baccalaureate Address

June 4, 1982

On this Commencement eve, I share with members of the Class of 1982 some thoughts about three Biblical metaphors related to tomorrow's graduation.

The first comparison looks at life as a journey. No journey has meaning, however, without the stopping-off places. If we were to fly non-stop around the world from Kennedy Airport to Kennedy Airport, the journey would have no meaning except perhaps as a kind of fake adventure. If we stop from time to time at distinctively different places, the journey begins to have significance, and we begin to understand what the trip is all about.

In our lives there are, similarly, stopping-off places that give meaning to the passage of time. When we are very, very young, our horizon is rarely further ahead than the next meal time. Then we begin to have a sense of birthdays and of Christmas as events that have special meaning and are worth looking forward to. Later on, the span grows longer, and we look forward to the time when we can have a driver's license, when we have a right to vote, and when we can drink a Miller Lite without looking out for the Housemaster.

Then come even more significant events. In my case it was putting on a uniform. I hope fervently that you never will. Then it may be marriage, followed probably by parenthood. No events are more profound and fulfilling than these. Someone in the Class of 1982 might even become a Head Master! Why not? Or a Pulitzer Prize-winning poet, a senator, a missionary, an industrial mogul, a Yosemite Valley Park ranger, or an admiral. Your predecessors—alumni who once fidgeted in these very same pews—have arrived during their journey through life at a great many different stopping-off places. So will you.

Commencement itself is a stopping-off place of traditional significance. As we gather here this evening, it is worth taking a few moments to look at the implications of this Commencement and of the journey image for our whole lives.

First of all, we are part of a time stream that we cannot avoid no matter how much we try. Though it is easy when we are watching television to switch from one station to another when we are displeased with the program or are restless with ourselves, the time stream that we live in has no such convenient switch. However much we may wish to return to some earlier era of supposed innocence or virtue, we are always locked in the iron embrace of the present. However much we may yearn for some future utopia, we ultimately know that any such yearning is a will-o'-the-wisp search for an unreachable finality. The present is all we have.

Similarly, events in the journey of life follow inexorably one from another. What we will be next week follows from what we are today. We cannot undo what we have already done. We cannot, as it were, rearrange our past to try to make the present more to our liking. The grades that your teachers turned in on Thursday measure a past that cannot be changed. So do the prizes that will be awarded tomorrow.

Though events follow inevitably from one another, it is clear that on our journey through life we have choices to make. Robert Frost's simple poem about choosing between two paths expresses the truth figuratively.

We can say with statistical confidence that the following events will take place within the remaining lives of the members of the Class of 1982. One-hundred-eighty-six of you will marry at least once. Sixty-two of those first marriages will end in divorce. Twenty of you will become alcoholics. Twelve of you will become teachers; twenty-eight will be managers. Two will become Lawrenceville Trustees and vote for or against coeducation!

What no one can predict at this time is who will be what statistic. Michel Quoist, the French worker-priest, asks, "What good are strong and agile legs if you don't know in which direction to run?" We might rephrase that to ask, "What good is a fine education if we don't know what choices to make?" We do have choices.

We will come back to the matter of choices a little later, but I cannot avoid this evening a further development of the journey image. All human history suggests that on our respective journeys, the unexpected nearly always has a way of happening. Do you suppose, for example, that those British soldiers and sailors now risking their lives in the South Atlantic could have even named the Falkland Islands six months ago? They have had no choice at all in the matter. It is a chilling thought that sometimes we have no choice at all over some things that we must face.

It is even more chilling to recognize that human beings all over the world increasingly are beginning to think that we are now in a position where the path for all of us—and for all succeeding generations—may come to an end with our lifetime. I myself have no doubt that if we plunge over the nuclear precipice, human life as we know it on this earth will inevitably come to an end. There will then be no more journeys or stopping-off places, or choices.

Let me turn now to a second image. As there are stopping-off places during journeys that give meaning to our travel, so there are times of flowering that give meaning to growth. When we plant an asparagus bed or a fruit tree, we look forward to the time when it will produce the good things that we hope we will be able to harvest, like Jersey asparagus in May, or Mackintosh apples in September.

A life has many flowerings, and this Commencement time is one of them. It is a happy time like blossom time in the Shenandoah Valley. The Class of 1982 thinks of it primarily as a flowering time of their own effort. A time when they receive a diploma as the reward for the growth that has taken place while they have been Lawrentians.

Is it not just as much a flowering time for parent and grandparent, for sister and cousin, for teacher and trustee, as it is for the Class of 1982?

One of the risks of thinking about this Commencement as a flowering time—as a culmination—is that we may think of it as an end to growth, whereas it is, in fact, just a part of growth. A parent of the member of the Class of 1982 has a different, but just as real sense of flowering as does anyone who will receive a diploma tomorrow. The parent has made a commitment of nurture that has helped the growth and results in the award of a diploma. So also has the teacher who has committed a lifetime to making a difference in the world and to helping young people come into maturity.

Not all trees bear good fruit, however, and we must—all of us—bear some of the responsibility. Just outside our New Hampshire farmhouse there is an old apple tree, misshapen, insect riddled, and slovenly in appearance. The nuthatches love it for its insects, but the fruit that it bears is inedible and full of cankers. In a word, the tree still lives, its leaves are green, but its fruit is useless. It has stopped growing.

So it is that human beings can continue to live long after they have stopped growing. Fear of the future can be a blight because it turns us to look only to the past and blinds us to new understandings of life. Unwillingness to accept the complexity of our lives can trap us into looking for easy answers. That's why the Moral Majority has such appeal to so many today. It provides easy answers to complex and perhaps unanswerable questions. Whenever we know we have absolutely the final answer, absolutely the final equation, that's when we know we have reached the end of growth: the end of life. No tree can be fruitful after it has stopped growing.

My final image has to do with building a house. You will remember that the wise, sensible man builds his house on rock, and it does not fall when the floods and the winds beat upon it. The foolish man, however, finds that his house collapses when the rain and the floods strike it.

How we make our way through life is not just a matter of recognizing our journey, or of remaining open to growth, but also a matter of building our lives on solid foundations of principle. Fortunately others have taken the trip before us, and others are also taking it with us. We need not depend entirely upon ourselves to have a sense of what is rock and what is sand.

Let's try a few aphorisms from the tradition of which we are part:

Man does not live by bread alone.

Absolute power corrupts absolutely.

Murder will out.

This above all: to thine own self be true.

Honor thy father and thy mother.

It is better to give than to receive.

Love thy neighbor as thyself.

As you will recognize, I have drawn from Greece, from Elizabethan England, from the Bible, from political commentary, and from drama. We need not stand alone as we look for the rock foundations on which to build.

I believe that most members of the Class of 1982 already have a sense of where to put down solid foundations. They probably would not have reached this Commencement if they had not already started to build a strong sense of values. Perhaps, therefore, it makes sense to look at some of the areas that are not quite so obvious, some of the areas that are helpful in building an enduring and growing life.

A sense of the beautiful in the arts, in nature, and in other human beings can be important in our journey through life. As I make that remark, I think of Ruskin's observation, "Remember that the most beautiful things in the world are the most useless; peacocks and lilies for instance."

It has been said that only humans laugh. I don't know whether that's true or not, but, if so, it is a way of saying that a sense of proportion about human affairs can be extraordinarily important in building one's life. We laugh at the clown because his nose is so bulbous red, and we see also the tear in his eye so that our heart throbs even as we ourselves have tears, and we laugh. We need a sense of humor.

We have a great need also to see beyond the next turning in our lives, to have a vision that is ever before us. It is not given to many of us to be great visionaries, but we can all keep our sights on the horizon.

Many years ago when I first started jogging, I found it rather slow going. Indeed it is still rather slow going and getting slower every year! In any event, a young Lawrentian came up beside me and said, "Don't look down at your feet. Look up at the sky. Look at the horizon. Then your head will be back and your chest will be out, and you will be able to move forward with more energy." That was wonderful advice, and I have tried to follow it ever since, even when I have sometimes had too big a lunch!

So it is that life is a journey during which growth takes place, if only it rests on the solid rock of human values.

Gentlemen of the Graduating Class: Commencement is a way stop, one of the flowering times in the journey of your lives. Though we cannot know what lies ahead, it is inexorably true that each step will follow from what has gone before and that you will undoubtedly meet surprises. You will have to make choices, and you will also grow so that you can experience new fruitfulness at each time in your life.

As you journey, as you grow, as you make choices, you will be doing so in the awareness that if anything is to last, it must be built upon a sound bedrock of principles. I hope, moreover, that you will also cultivate a sense of the beautiful, a sense of humor, and a larger, longer vision for yourself than you might at first think possible.

I hope you have learned something about reading, writing, and arithmetic at Lawrenceville. I hope that you have also learned something about living with other human beings because that is the essential nature of a residential school experience. I hope finally that you have learned something about the difference between bedrock and sand.

Unseen realms lie ahead. May your journey be worthwhile, long lasting, adventurous, creative, and rewarding.

God bless us all.

—From the Baccalaureate Address

January 23, 1986

I've never had a busier year at Lawrenceville. Planning for coeducation and for the implementation of a new curriculum have both involved all sorts of new and interesting responsibilities. In a way, I wish that I were continuing as Head Master because I feel so positive about the future of our school.

As the Class of 1986 knows, this will be our last full year in Foundation House. Some say to us that it must be sad to think of leaving Lawrenceville. I am glad that people feel that way because it means that they are thinking of our many happy and fulfilled times on this campus.

But I, myself, prefer to think that this is not so much a sad time as a sentimental time. Mrs. McClellan and I care very much for Lawrenceville, a community in which we have had all kinds of experiences since our arrival in September, 1950. Our three children were born and raised here. We went through Korea and Viet Nam. We experienced the student unrest in the late 60's and early 70's, as well as the subsequent years of extraordinary inflation.

Through thick and thin, we have felt that our life and work here have been worthwhile. We have felt as well that our colleagues and all those with whom we have worked have been wonderfully supportive.

Not least, we have drawn strength from our relationships with young people. As they have grown in skills, in stature, and in moral strength, so we have felt that we have played some small part in contributing not only to the Lawrentians with whom we have been directly involved, but also, in a larger sense, to all young Americans growing to manhood.

As I think about young people growing up, I think particularly about the Class of 1986. Though I could mention by name student leaders, athletes, actors, characters, and others who are making this year unique, I prefer to say in a more general way that this year's Fifth Form seems to me distinctive as a whole for its pleasant common sense, for its openness and friendliness, and for its diligence and caring. The class began its Fifth Form year with good notices. It has lived up to its reputation and has added lustre in many ways during the year.

Now Lawrenceville is embarking on a new course, and the responsibility of planning for coeducation and for a new curriculum is both demanding and exhilarating. How wonderful it is to think at the end of one phase of our life that the institution to which we have committed so much of our energy is in fact poised for an entirely new phase of growth.

So it is that, as the Fifth Form gathers for the last time just before Commencement, Lawrentians can be proud of what they have accomplished, recognizing also that there have been ups and downs along the way. So it is also that Lawrentians gathering just before Commencement can feel a sense of forward momentum—of looking ahead—to college, family, and a creative life within our national society. So it is that at the conclusion of the school year there is perhaps some sadness, and certainly much sentiment, but the overwhelming feeling is of being ready for new challenges and for new responsibilities.

Though I write these words in early January because of a printer's inexorable demands, I will risk saying that the text for my Baccalaureate Address in June will come from Genesis, the first book of the Bible, the first chapter. "God created the world and saw that it was good." What that means to me is not that the world is without evils, sadnesses, conflict, and things that ought not to be. It means that our world is made up of all those experiences with the overarching knowledge that if we can share together we can inevitably grow; if we stick to our guns in terms of our human responsibilities, the outcomes will be good; and that a sound value system will lead to a worthwhile life. These are the thoughts that I have in mind as I think of my future and of yours in this last year of our tenure in Foundation House.

I conclude with the final word from our school motto. "Growing" is the key word. Lawrenceville is growing, Mary Elizabeth and Bruce McClellan are growing, the Class of 1986 is growing. We are all part of God's continuing creation.

God bless us one and all.

—From the Head Master's Olla Podrida *message*

June 5, 1986

Thank you, Tom, for that lovely introduction. I am reminded of an old aphorism: "the excesses of flattery never quite meet the expectations of conceit."

This is my thirty-sixth Lawrenceville faculty dinner, and it is my last as Head Master. We now expect Si Bunting to arrive for the spring term next year, and perhaps I can join you then as an *emeritus* faculty member. Some of you, I know, have been puzzled by the delay in Si's arrival, and it is appropriate for me to offer a brief explanation this evening. Perhaps I can explain things most simply by telling you that I called the Chairman of the Search Committee at Hampden-Sydney a couple of weeks ago and asked him what was holding things up? "Well," he responded, "it's taking us much longer than we had expected. We're looking for someone who is under forty, and who rode with General Lee."

In the course of thirty-six, year-end Lawrenceville dinners, I suppose I've heard a hundred or more valedictories, and as I have thought about this evening I have been trying to see if there is any pattern that could serve as a guide for my remarks on this occasion.

One model would be Abe Lincoln's marvelous seventy-three minute disquisition on the virtues of objective testing. Yes, we really did have an Abe Lincoln who was a member of the faculty. Yes, he really did speak more than an hour about testing at a year-end faculty dinner. No, that is not a model that I shall follow.

Then I thought of some fun evenings we have had. I thought perhaps of reminding us all of some of the rich lore of faculty nicknames. Who can tell me who was called "Carbonlung"? Who can tell me who was "The B of Buchenwald"? Who can tell me who is "Chrome Dome"? And by the way, what is all this business about "Rhubarb"? I haven't quite got that one figured out!

To tell the truth, I collected a long list of current faculty nicknames thinking that I might have fun with them this evening. Over a period of several weeks at my Fifth Form luncheon table, I explored the present underground nomenclature for faculty members. Some of what I came up with is mentionable; some is not. It eventually seemed, however, that it would be the better part of wisdom not to share those nicknames with everyone this evening. After all, I might really come back next June as an *emeritus* attendee.

Then, in a tenderer mood, I began thinking about reminiscences: Frank Heyniger's wonderful sense of humor, Ed Megna's practical jokes, and Carty Lynch's "ah bon." Those memories are very much part of my life, and I count them gifts, but could not see how to weave them into this occasion.

So I have finally settled for something rather less than Lincoln's Gettysburg Address. I have decided simply to share with my colleagues some brief reminiscences of my own.

It all began for us in February, 1950, when Mary Elizabeth and I arrived in a driving rainstorm on the doorstep of Gladys and Larry Tiihonen's Raymond House apartment. The campus was as baffling to a stranger then as it is now, and we thought that when we had crossed the Hudson River from Williamstown, Massachusetts, there was a certain danger of ambush from Indians. Eventually, we arrived at Foundation House to stay with Allan and Pattie Heely, and eventually we were offered a teaching appointment in the English department.

I came to Lawrenceville because it seemed to me to offer a first-class professional opportunity in the classroom. Tom Johnson, of Emily Dickinson fame, was then chairman of the department, and a listing of those who were then teaching in the department would be a roster of those who taught me how to teach English.

Nine years later, we moved into Foundation House with a new title. As I think many of you know, I am inordinately proud of the Lawrenceville title of Head Master with two words. Meaning that at Lawrenceville the Head Master is simply the teacher who has a somewhat more extended range of responsibility than other teachers.

I was 35 then. Like many young persons, I thought I knew a good many of the answers to the questions of the time. In fact, I can remember sitting in the Hamill House living room and thinking to myself that I could solve most of the School's problems in thirty minutes with ten quick decisions. Moving 150 yards across to the other side of the gate changed my perspective entirely. That was one of the important learning experiences of my life. If you are where the buck stops, the perspective is different.

Learning about that new perspective took a little time. A couple of years later, Ted Graham, then teaching at the Thacher School in California, accepted a Lawrenceville appointment. He was looking forward to his arrival in New Jersey when a Thacher colleague reported to him that, "the new young head at Lawrenceville is awful; everyone hates him." Well, Ted stayed and so have I.

Over the years I have collected various comments about what it is like to be a Head Master. Here's one: "Being the head of a school is like being stoned to death with marshmallows." Here's another: "What a Head Master learns is that a school is a group of principalities held together by a common heating system."

But I'd rather not talk this evening about being Head Master. I prefer to talk about being a master: an English teacher. Many of you have heard me say that I regard teaching as the finest—if not the oldest—of professions. There is a bonding together of those who teach. Nowhere is it expressed more directly than by Chaucer's Clerk of Oxenford, "And gladly would he learn, and gladly teach."

When I said in chapel at the spring assembly last Saturday morning that I was the person who was grateful for the privilege of being allowed to be part of the lives of young people growing up, I meant it. I also felt then a kind of infilling of my own spirit even at this September time of my life. Last Saturday I said to students that I doubted they could understand what I meant by that, and I'm not even certain that all of my faculty colleagues can understand it as I do now, but I cherish for you the hope that one day every one of us in this room will have had that powerful feeling.

There's an element of the moralist in all that Senator Sam Ervin once observed about himself, something that I also feel. He said, "I suffer from earth's worst affliction, a Scotch-Irish Presbyterian conscience, which commands me to act in accordance with my convictions." There is something deeply moral about teaching; it's so much more than training puppy dogs not to stain the living room rug.

Robert Graves observed years ago that "the writing of good English is a moral matter." I believe that absolutely. In that sense, I see teaching as essentially a moral occupation.

Let me be clear on that point. Though in a sense the English teacher and the history teacher have a special responsibility within the specifics of their discipline, I believe that the great strength of the liberal arts tradition lies in a moral core of commitment, of diligence, of unflinching honesty, of objective inquiring, and of sensibility to the infinite capabilities of each student and each fellow worker.

Let me carry that general line of thought just a bit further. I believe that our deepest yearning as human beings is to become immortal. When we touch the life of a young person growing up, we give that person part of us that continues on and beyond us through all time. It may not be a very large part, it may not be a very visible part. It may not even be something that we ourselves recognize, but when we have given something of ourselves to another person we have, in fact, achieved a kind of immortality.

If I have done nothing else as Head Master, I hope that I have at least sustained the dignity of a career in teaching and the divinity of the young whom we teach.

So it is that here this evening I feel not that I am being honored but that I am honoring my colleagues. I close with a quote from Lao-tse on leadership:

A leader is best when people barely know he exists.
Not so good when people obey and acclaim him.
Worse when they despise him.
But of a good leader
who talks little
When this work is done
His aim fulfilled
They will say: "We did it ourselves."

—From remarks made at the Faculty Dinner